No Love Lost:

The Theory of Conservation of Love

Dr Jawahar Surisetti

Copyright © 2024

Dr Jawahar Surisetti

All rights reserved. This book or any portion thereof may not be reproduced or used in any manner whatsoever without the express written permission of the publisher except for the use of brief quotations in a book review.

First printing, 2024.

Acknowledgements to my parents ,
Sujata my wife , Jayesh , Jagrit , Neha
and Jaishna- the little one .

Introduction

Navigating the Currents of Love

In the vast and tumultuous sea of human experience, love stands as the prevailing current that propels us forward, molds our identities, and forges connections that transcend boundaries. "No Love Lost: The Theory of Conservation of Love" is your quintessential navigational tool, offering a deep dive into the essence of love and its pivotal role at every echelon of human engagement. Written by the acclaimed futurist and psychologist Dr Jawahar Surisetti, it's his theory that is both shocking as well as scientific . He covers the psychology and science of love like never before.

At the heart of our personal universe, this enlightening tome acts as a beacon, illuminating the complex mechanics of love in our private spheres. It dissects the psychological foundations of love, the emotional ties that bind us to kin, comrades, and companions of the heart, and the intricate equilibrium required to nurture each of these precious bonds. The Theory of Conservation of Love posits a revolutionary idea: our capacity for love is not boundless but a treasured commodity to be stewarded with care, ensuring every relationship is cherished and sustained.

On a grander scale, the book ventures into how love's tenets resonate within the vast expanse of societal and international arenas. Nations, much like individuals, must deftly manage their emotional reserves, balancing a labyrinth of alliances, economic partnerships, and diplomatic interactions. In this context, love transforms into a symbol for the benevolence and esteem nations exchange, a resource that demands strategic distribution to foster global concord.

Delving into the psychology of love, the book draws upon cutting-edge research to shed light on how our formative years, cultural milieu, and personal narratives sculpt our approach to love's give and take. It unveils recurring motifs in our love narratives and equips us with introspective tools for personal evolution.

"No Love Lost: The Theory of Conservation of Love" transcends the realm of scholarly discourse to become an indispensable guide for anyone yearning to deepen their comprehension of love. Whether you're a psychology aficionado, a professional steering through the complexities of international relations, or an individual aspiring to enrich your personal connections, this book imparts invaluable insights, empowering you to allocate your love in ways that yield happiness and fulfilment.

As we set sail through the enlightening pages of "No Love Lost," we encourage you to embrace a novel perspective on love. Allow this volume to steer you as you navigate the depths of your own heart and the expansive world beyond, uncovering the infinite possibilities that love, in all its myriad forms, has to offer.

Prologue: The Constancy of the Heart

In a world awash with relentless change, where each tick of the clock ushers in a novel challenge, there remains a steadfast beacon – the human heart's unyielding capacity to love. This perpetual force is the cornerstone of our collective narratives, a silent yet potent energy that intertwines with the fabric of our existence, uniting us in an eternal ballet as timeless as the cosmos.

Yet, amidst the whirlwind of contemporary life, we are confronted with a dilemma as ancient as humanity itself: the distribution of our finite emotional wealth, love. Could it be that, akin to the laws of energy conservation in physics, there's an analogous axiom at play within the realm of our feelings? This intriguing notion is the essence of the Theory of Conservation of Love.

Embark on a voyage through the intricacies of the human spirit, as we dissect the allocation of our affections among the diverse bonds that sculpt our identity – from familial ties to romantic entanglements, from friendships to national allegiance. This odyssey seeks to map the immeasurable, to impose order upon the ebb and flow of our passions, and to comprehend the equilibrium we must maintain as we invest fragments of our essence into others.

As we traverse the chapters ahead, we'll engage with the arithmetic of affection, the societal frameworks that mould our viewpoints, and the destiny of love in a perpetually transforming world. We'll encounter narratives of love's reallocation, confront objections to the theory, and unearth actionable insights that can steer us toward a more balanced coexistence.

Welcome to a narrative that defies the conventional, a dialogue that fuses the heart with the intellect, and a conversation that echoes in the depths of the soul. Welcome to the "Theory of Conservation of Love".

Chapter 1: The Fundamental Law of Love

Introduction to the Concept of Love as a Quantifiable Entity

In the quest to comprehend the complexities of human emotion, love has perennially emerged as an enigmatic force, often eluding the grasp of concrete definition and measurement. Yet, in this seminal chapter, we embark on an intellectual odyssey to demystify love, proposing the audacious notion that it can indeed be quantified and recognized as a constant entity within the tapestry of an individual's existence. By dissecting the multifaceted dimensions of love, we aim to establish a foundational framework that allows for a systematic exploration of its influence and manifestations in human life.

The Multidimensional Nature of Love

Love, as we propose, is not a monolithic construct but a constellation of emotions, actions, and states of being that coalesce into a dynamic and powerful force. It transcends mere affection or attraction, encompassing a spectrum that includes altruism, compassion, empathy, and a profound sense of connection. To quantify love, we must first acknowledge its multidimensional nature, dissecting it into measurable components such as intensity, duration, and impact on well-being. This approach enables us to apply empirical methodologies to what was once considered the exclusive domain of poets and philosophers.

The Constancy of Love Across Time and Space

Contrary to the popular belief that love is fleeting and capricious, our thesis posits that love, in its essence, maintains a remarkable constancy across time and space. This constancy is not to suggest that love is static or unchanging, but rather that its presence in an individual's life exhibits a persistent and enduring quality. Through longitudinal studies and cross-cultural analyses, we can observe patterns and commonalities that suggest love's fundamental role in human development and societal cohesion.

Love as a Driving Force in Human Behavior

The influence of love on human behavior is both profound and pervasive. It acts as a catalyst for actions that range from the mundane to the extraordinary, shaping decisions and guiding ethical considerations. Love's role as a motivational force can be quantified through its outcomes—be it in acts of charity, the pursuit of justice, or the nurturing of family and community bonds. By examining these outcomes, we can begin to measure the weight of love's influence on individual and collective actions.

Methodological Approaches to Quantifying Love

To quantify love, we must employ a diverse array of methodological approaches that honor its complexity. This includes qualitative methods that capture the subjective experiences of love, as well as quantitative measures that seek to provide objective data on its effects. Psychological assessments, sociological surveys, and even neuroscientific investigations all contribute to a more holistic understanding of love's quantifiable aspects. Through these methods, we can construct a more nuanced and robust portrait of love's role in human life.

Embracing the Quantifiable Aspects of Love

This serves as a clarion call to embrace the possibility of quantifying love, to recognize it as a fundamental law that governs human interaction and personal fulfilment. By approaching love with the rigour of academic inquiry, we can shed light on its mechanisms and effects, thereby enriching our understanding of this most cherished human experience. As we continue to explore the dimensions of love, we lay the foundation for a new era of research that honors the depth and breadth of this universal phenomenon.

Defining Love as a Quantifiable Entity

Love, an emotion as old as humanity itself, has been the subject of poetry, art, and philosophy throughout the ages. Yet, despite its ubiquity in human culture, love has largely eluded the grasp of empirical measurement and scientific scrutiny. In this discourse, we propose a novel perspective: love as a quantifiable entity. This approach does not seek to reduce the richness of love to mere numbers but aims to enhance our understanding of its dynamics and distribution in interpersonal relationships.

The Quantification of Love: A Theoretical Framework

The concept of quantifying love may seem counterintuitive at first glance. Love is often described as an ineffable feeling, transcending the boundaries of rational explanation. However, by drawing parallels with the principles of energy in physics, we can begin to conceptualize love as a measurable force. Energy, in its various forms, can be converted, transferred, and conserved. Similarly, love can be thought of as an emotional energy that is exchanged between individuals, capable of transformation and conservation.

Measuring Love: Attention, Time, and Emotional Investment

To quantify love, we must identify its constituent components. Three primary dimensions emerge as quantifiable aspects of love: attention, time, and emotional investment. Attention, the focus we give to our loved ones, can be measured in the frequency and quality of our interactions. Time, the most finite of resources, is a clear indicator of our priorities and can be quantified in hours and minutes spent with loved ones. Emotional investment, though more complex, can be gauged through the depth of our feelings and the extent of our commitment and sacrifices for another person.

The Distribution of Love Among Relationships

Just as energy is allocated among various systems, love is distributed among our relationships. This distribution is not uniform; it varies based on the nature and intensity of each relationship. Familial love, romantic love, and platonic love each command a different share of our emotional resources. By recognizing this, we can begin to understand the patterns of our emotional expenditures and the balance, or imbalance, that may exist within our personal networks.

The Implications of Quantifying Love

The implications of quantifying love are profound. It allows for a more objective analysis of relationships and provides a framework for understanding the dynamics of human connection. For instance, by quantifying the love in a relationship, individuals can assess whether their emotional needs are being met and whether they are investing their emotional energy wisely. Furthermore, therapists and counselors can use these metrics to help individuals and couples understand and improve their relationships.

Challenges and Limitations

While the quantification of love offers intriguing possibilities, it is not without its challenges and limitations. Love is a multifaceted and dynamic emotion, influenced by a myriad of factors including cultural norms, personal experiences, and biological predispositions. Quantitative measures may not capture the full spectrum of love's expression and could oversimplify its complexity. Additionally, the subjective nature of emotional investment means that what constitutes a significant investment for one person may be different for another.

The notion of love as a quantifiable entity opens up new avenues for exploring the most cherished of human emotions. By considering love in terms of attention, time, and emotional investment, we can begin to approach it with the same rigor as any other aspect of human behavior. While we must be cautious not to lose sight of love's inherent mystery and depth, quantifying love can provide valuable insights into the workings of our hearts and the nature of our connections with others. As we continue to explore this concept, we may find that love, in all its complexity, can indeed be measured, understood, and perhaps even more deeply appreciated.

The Equation of Love: A Heart's Tender Algebra

Takeaway : In the arithmetic of the heart, it's often believed that our capacity to love is not boundless. Like the finite resources of time and energy, the love we have to offer is thought to be a quantifiable sum that we allocate across the various relationships in our lives.

In an attempt to quantify the unquantifiable, let's consider the following formula, a simple yet profound equation that seeks to capture the essence of our emotional investments:

$$L_{total} = L_{mother} + L_{partner} + L_{others} = \text{Constant}$$

This equation suggests that the total amount of love one can give (L_{total}) is a fixed value, much like a pie that can be sliced in various ways but never increases in size. The love shared with a mother (L_{mother}), a partner ($L_{partner}$), and others in our lives (L_{others}) is divided from this constant sum, implying that to give more to one may require giving less to another.

However, this equation, while neat and tidy, might be too simplistic to encapsulate the depth and complexity of human emotions. Love, after all, is not a commodity to be measured and parcelled out but a dynamic and evolving force. It's not uncommon to hear stories of hearts growing larger, capable of more love than one ever thought possible, especially when life introduces new relationships or deepens existing ones.

In the end, the Equation of Love is less about strict mathematics and more about the philosophical pondering of how we choose to prioritize our affections. It's a reminder that while our time and attention are limited, the human heart's capacity for love might just be more elastic than we imagine. Perhaps the true takeaway is not that love is finite, but that it is our responsibility to nurture it, allowing it to grow and encompass all those we hold dear.

Historical Perspectives on the Constancy of Love

Throughout the ages, love has been a central theme in the human experience, often depicted as a force of immeasurable power and infinite abundance. Yet, there's a fascinating contrast in the way different cultures and historical periods have conceptualized love's capacity. This exploration takes us on a journey through time, examining the notion that love, rather than being boundless, might have been seen as a finite treasure to be guarded and distributed with care.

Love as a Limited Commodity

In many ancient societies, love was often portrayed as a precious resource, much like water in a desert. The Greeks, for example, had a variety of words for love, each representing a different kind—ranging from the passionate Eros to the deep familial bonds of Storge. This categorization suggests a nuanced understanding that love, in its various forms, was something to be allocated judiciously among different relationships. Similarly, in medieval chivalric traditions, a knight's devotion to a lady was an exclusive and all-consuming affair, implying that his capacity for romantic love was wholly invested in a single person.

Cultural Narratives and Love's Boundaries

Moving through the tapestry of time, we find that many cultural narratives have echoed this sentiment. In some Eastern philosophies, the idea of balance and harmony within relationships often hints at a careful distribution of emotional energy. Love, in this context, is not just an emotion but a responsibility that requires a mindful approach. Contrastingly, the Victorian era brought with it a romantic idealism that still influences contemporary views. Yet, even within this idealism, there was an undercurrent of restraint—a belief that one's heart could be given only once and that love, once bestowed, was an irrevocable pledge.

Modern Reflections on Love's Infinity

Today, we often hear that love knows no bounds—that it is an infinite resource we can give without depletion. This modern perspective encourages the expression of love in its many forms, without fear of running out. We celebrate the idea that one can love multiple people, in various ways, all at once. Yet, even now, we encounter situations where love feels strained or limited, suggesting that perhaps our capacity for emotional investment has practical limits.

Embracing Love's Rich Tapestry

As we reflect on these historical perspectives, it becomes clear that love's constancy is a complex tapestry woven with threads of culture, philosophy, and personal belief. Whether seen as a finite commodity or an infinite wellspring, love remains a fundamental part of the human condition. By understanding the diverse ways in which love has been perceived throughout history, we can appreciate its multifaceted nature and the unique ways it enriches our lives today. Love, in all its forms, continues to evolve, but its significance in our stories and experiences remains as steadfast as ever.

Balancing the Scales of Affection

Navigating the waters of new relationships often means learning to reallocate our emotional investments. When we welcome a significant other into our lives, it's like adding another dish to an already delicate set of scales. This chapter delves into the intricate process of redistributing our affection, ensuring that our love is spread evenly without the possibility of adding more to the finite reserve we hold. It's a dance of give-and-take, a recalibration of the heart's capacity to care for those we hold dear.

The Redistribution of Love

Imagine your heart as a garden, where each person in your life is a plant that you nurture and care for. The arrival of a spouse or partner is akin to planting a new, demanding species that requires a significant share of your attention and resources. This doesn't mean that the other plants should wither; rather, it's about finding a new equilibrium. The chapter explores strategies for maintaining the health of the entire garden, ensuring that each plant continues to thrive. It's about recognizing that while the quantity of love remains constant, the quality of our attention and care can make all the difference.

The Emotional Budget

Just as a financial budget helps us manage our monetary resources, an emotional budget can guide us in the stewardship of our affections. This section of the chapter encourages readers to take stock of their emotional expenditures and make conscious decisions about where to invest their time and energy. It's about setting priorities, establishing boundaries, and sometimes making tough choices for the greater good of all relationships involved. By doing so, we can prevent emotional debt and nurture a balanced, fulfilling network of connections.

Nurturing Existing Bonds

While the excitement of a new relationship can be all-consuming, it's crucial to remember the value of the bonds we've built over time. This part of the chapter offers practical advice on how to continue cherishing and strengthening existing relationships, even as we make room for new ones. It's about the art of multitasking with a heart, where we learn to be present for our loved ones in meaningful ways, despite the demands of our newest commitments. It's a reminder that every relationship, old or new, deserves its own spotlight.

Embracing Change with Grace

Change is an inevitable part of life, and the way we handle it can define the quality of our relationships. This final section of the chapter is a heartfelt guide to embracing the ebb and flow of affection with grace and resilience. It's about understanding that as we grow and evolve, so too do our relationships. By staying flexible and open-hearted, we can balance the scales of affection, ensuring that love is not just a finite resource to be allocated, but a dynamic force that grows and transforms with us.

The journey of balancing the scales of affection is a continuous one, filled with learning and adaptation. As we navigate the complexities of new relationships, we must be mindful of the delicate balance that keeps our emotional ecosystem thriving. By thoughtfully redistributing our love, maintaining an emotional budget, nurturing existing bonds, and embracing change with grace, we can achieve a harmonious balance that enriches every connection in our lives.

Love's Conservation in Practice

Love, much like energy in the physical world, is neither created nor destroyed; it merely transforms and adapts to the shifting dynamics of our relationships and circumstances. The conservation of love is a concept that can be observed in the everyday actions and decisions we make, often without even realizing it. This article delves into the practical ways in which we subconsciously balance and maintain the love in our lives, ensuring that it endures through the ebbs and flows of life's constant changes.

Recognizing Love's Adaptability

Love is not a static emotion; it is dynamic and malleable, changing form to suit the needs of the moment. For instance, the passionate love of a new relationship often evolves into a deeper, more stable connection over time. This transformation is a natural conservation of love, as the initial intensity is not sustainable indefinitely. Instead, it matures into a form that is more conducive to long-term companionship, demonstrating love's incredible ability to adapt to the stages of our lives.

Balancing Acts in Relationships

In any relationship, there are moments of give and take that exemplify love's conservation. When one partner is going through a tough time, the other often steps up, providing additional support and understanding. This is not a one-way street; the roles will inevitably reverse at some point, with the initial giver becoming the receiver of support. This reciprocal dynamic ensures that the overall balance of love and care within the relationship is maintained, even as individual contributions fluctuate.

Love's Presence in Daily Decisions

The conservation of love is also evident in the small, seemingly inconsequential decisions we make every day. Choosing to send a thoughtful message, making time for a shared meal, or simply listening attentively when your partner speaks are all ways in which we conserve and nurture the love in our relationships. These actions might seem minor, but they are the building blocks of a resilient, loving bond that can withstand the tests of time and change.

Nurturing Love Through Challenges

Life is full of challenges that can strain even the strongest of relationships. However, it is precisely through these challenges that the conservation of love is most critical. By facing difficulties together, partners can strengthen their bond, learning to conserve their love by focusing on what truly matters. This might mean forgiving small grievances, compromising on issues, or finding new ways to connect and support each other. Through these practices, love is not only conserved but also enriched.

The Enduring Cycle of Love

Ultimately, the conservation of love is an ongoing process, a cycle of actions and reactions that continuously shape our relationships. It requires mindfulness and intentionality, a willingness to adapt, and a commitment to balance. By recognizing the importance of conserving love in practice, we can foster relationships that are resilient, fulfilling, and capable of withstanding the inevitable changes that life brings. Love, in its many forms, remains one of the most powerful forces in our lives, and its conservation is a testament to its enduring significance.

Exploring the Boundaries of Affection: A Path to Personal Development

In the journey of self-improvement, the concept of love's conservation emerges as a pivotal understanding that can transform our interpersonal dynamics. This profound realization not only enriches our emotional intelligence but also paves the way for more harmonious and fulfilling relationships. By delving into the essence of love's finite nature, we unlock the potential for significant personal growth and a deeper connection with those around us.

The Finite Nature of Love: A Catalyst for Mindful Relationships

It's a common misconception that love, in its many forms, is an inexhaustible resource. However, the truth is that our emotional bandwidth and energy are limited. Acknowledging this limitation is not a sign of love's weakness but rather a testament to its value. When we understand that our capacity to love is not boundless, we begin to prioritize our emotional investments more wisely, fostering relationships that are both meaningful and sustainable.

Prioritization: The Key to Nurturing Significant Bonds

With the awareness that our love is a precious commodity, we learn to be more selective with our affections. This discernment encourages us to invest in relationships that truly resonate with our values and aspirations. By doing so, we not only enhance the quality of our connections but also ensure that our emotional energy is directed towards nurturing bonds that have the potential to thrive and stand the test of time.

Emotional Budgeting: Balancing the Scales of Affection

Just as we budget our finances to ensure stability and growth, so too must we budget our emotional resources. This concept of 'emotional budgeting' allows us to allocate our love and attention where it's most needed, preventing the depletion of our emotional reserves. By managing our affections with intention, we create a balanced and healthy emotional ecosystem that supports our well-being and the well-being of those we care about.

The Ripple Effect: Personal Growth and Beyond

The implications of love's conservation extend far beyond our immediate relationships. As we become more attuned to the ebb and flow of our emotional capacities, we experience a ripple effect of growth. This personal evolution is characterized by increased self-awareness, empathy, and resilience. We become better equipped to navigate life's challenges and more adept at cultivating a supportive network of relationships that enrich our lives.

Embracing Love's Conservation for a Fulfilling Life

The recognition of love's conservation is a transformative concept that holds the key to personal growth and relationship fulfillment. By embracing this understanding, we open ourselves up to a world of deeper connections and heightened self-awareness. As we journey through life, let us remember that the conservation of love is not a limitation but a guiding principle that can lead us to a more harmonious and satisfying existence.

Chapter 2: The Heart of the Home: Nurturing Love in Personal Relationships

In the warm embrace of family life, love acts as the cornerstone that holds relationships together. This chapter explores the rich tapestry of affection that binds the family unit, illuminating the subtle shifts that occur when new members are woven into the fabric. We'll examine the dynamics of love as it evolves from the sweet simplicity of a couple's bond to the complex, multifaceted connections within an extended family. Through stories and insights, we'll uncover the ways in which love's expression adapts, ensuring that each individual feels cherished and integral to the family mosaic.

As we navigate the ebb and flow of daily life, the introduction of new family members—be it through birth, marriage, or other means—presents opportunities for love to expand and deepen. This chapter offers guidance on fostering an environment where love can flourish, even amidst the challenges of change. We'll share strategies for maintaining harmony and strengthening bonds, celebrating the unique contributions of each person. Join us on a journey to discover how love, in its many forms, is the glue that holds the heart of the home together.

The Dynamics of Love Distribution in Families: A Fluid and Evolving Landscape

Love within a family is like a living, breathing entity, constantly in motion and evolving with the ebb and flow of life's changes. It's a force that binds us, a silent language spoken through actions and felt through presence. In this exploration, we delve into the intricate dance of love's distribution among family members, a dance that is as fluid as it is profound.

The Initial Weave of Love's Tapestry

At the heart of every family lies an initial pattern of love distribution, a foundational weave that sets the tone for relationships. This pattern is often established early on, as parents pour their love into their children, siblings form bonds, and each member finds their unique place within the family unit. This initial distribution is characterized by a pure, unadulterated affection that is both nurturing and protective.

The Ripple Effect of New Bonds

As families grow and evolve, so too does the distribution of love. The introduction of new members—be it through marriages, partnerships, or the birth of children—creates ripples in the existing dynamic. Each new bond has the potential to redistribute love in unexpected ways, expanding the family's emotional landscape. This isn't a zero-sum game; rather, love multiplies, creating more to share and experience.

The Ebb and Flow of Life's Seasons

Life's inevitable changes—such as children growing up and leaving the nest, or elders passing on—also reshape the contours of love within a family. These transitions can be challenging, as they require a recalibration of emotional investments and the roles individuals play. Yet, they also offer opportunities for growth and deepening of connections, as family members learn to support each other in new ways.

Navigating the Complex Currents

Navigating the complex currents of love's distribution is no small feat. It requires empathy, communication, and a willingness to adapt. Families must recognize that each member's need for love and support can vary greatly depending on life's circumstances. It's a delicate balance, ensuring that everyone feels valued and cared for, while also allowing for individual expression and autonomy.

The Unending Journey of Love

Ultimately, the distribution of love within a family is an unending journey, one that doesn't have a final destination but rather a series of milestones and memories. It's a journey marked by laughter and tears, triumphs and trials, but above all, it's a journey fueled by the unwavering force of love. As families continue to navigate this complex terrain, they create a legacy of love that transcends time and becomes the bedrock of their shared history.

The dynamics of love distribution in families are as diverse and complex as the families themselves. It's a fluid process that adapts to the ever-changing landscape of relationships and life events. By understanding and embracing this fluidity, families can foster a deeper sense of connection and belonging that endures through all of life's seasons.

Love Transference: Navigating the Heart's Journey from Parental to Marital Bonds

Love is an ever-evolving emotion, a journey that transforms and adapts as we navigate through life's different stages. One of the most profound shifts in the landscape of love occurs as we transition from the protective embrace of our parents to the intimate partnership of marriage. This chapter delves into the intricate psychological metamorphosis that accompanies this pivotal life change, exploring how the deep-seated love for parental figures is reallocated to a spouse, and the implications this has on our emotional well-being and the nature of our relationships.

The Emotional Tapestry of Love: Weaving New Bonds

As children, our first experience of love is typically through the bond we share with our parents or primary caregivers. This foundational relationship sets the stage for our understanding of love, trust, and security. However, as we grow and step into the world of romantic relationships, culminating in marriage, there is a subtle yet significant reallocation of emotional investment. The chapter investigates this transition, shedding light on how the love once solely reserved for parental figures is now shared with a marital partner. This redistribution is not a simple transfer; it is a complex process of weaving new emotional patterns while honoring the old.

The Psychology Behind the Shift: Understanding the Dynamics

The transition from parental love to marital love is not merely a change in direction of affection but involves a psychological transformation. This section of the chapter examines the dynamics of this shift, considering factors such as attachment styles, the influence of family dynamics, and the individual's emotional maturity. It is through understanding these elements that we can appreciate the delicate balance required to maintain healthy relationships with both parental figures and a spouse. The psychological shift is a dance of closeness and distance, as we learn to navigate the boundaries of these distinct yet interconnected forms of love.

The Ripple Effect: Consequences on Relationships

The redistribution of love from parents to a spouse does not occur in isolation; it has a ripple effect on the individual's broader network of relationships. This part of the chapter explores the consequences of love transference on the relationship with parents, the marital bond, and even the potential future relationship with one's own children. It is a testament to the interconnectedness of human relationships and the importance of managing this transition with care and mindfulness. The way we handle this shift can set the tone for the health and resilience of our relationships for years to come.

Nurturing the Bonds: Strategies for a Smooth Transition

Acknowledging the challenges and complexities of love transference, this chapter offers practical strategies to facilitate a smoother transition from parental to marital bonds. It emphasizes the importance of open communication, self-awareness, and setting healthy boundaries. By actively nurturing both sets of relationships, individuals can create a balanced emotional ecosystem where love can flourish in all its forms. This section provides guidance on how to honor the past while embracing the future, ensuring that love's journey is one of growth and fulfilment.

Embracing the Evolution of Love

The journey of love from the cradle of parental care to the shared life of marriage is a testament to the adaptive nature of the human heart. As we close this chapter, we reflect on the beauty and complexity of love's evolution. The transference of love is not a loss but a redistribution that enriches our lives, allowing us to experience love's depth and breadth in new and profound ways. By understanding and navigating this transition with grace and intention, we can strengthen our bonds and revel in the transformative power of love.

In the end, love's true essence lies in its ability to adapt and grow, shaping our lives and relationships in its ever-changing embrace. Whether we are turning to our parents or our partners, love remains the guiding force that connects us, teaches us, and ultimately, defines us.

Balancing Love: Navigating Affection Among Siblings, Friends, and Extended Family

Love is a multifaceted emotion that extends beyond the romantic sphere, touching the lives of siblings, friends, and extended family members. As we embark on new intimate relationships, the delicate equilibrium of affection we share with these important individuals can be challenged. It's essential to navigate these waters with care and consideration to maintain the harmony and health of all our relationships.

The Sibling Connection: Preserving Bonds Amidst New Love

Siblings often share a unique bond, forged through shared experiences and a deep understanding of each other's quirks and qualities. When a new romantic relationship enters the scene, it's crucial to ensure that siblings don't feel sidelined or neglected.

- **Prioritize Quality Time**: Set aside regular one-on-one time with your siblings to catch up and engage in activities you both enjoy. This consistent effort shows that, despite your new relationship, they remain a priority in your life.

- **Communicate Openly**: Be honest with your siblings about your new commitments but reassure them of their importance to you. Open communication can prevent misunderstandings and feelings of abandonment.

- **Involve Them**: Where appropriate, involve your siblings in your new relationship. Introducing them to your partner can help integrate your worlds and foster a sense of inclusion.

The Art of Friendship: Balancing Old and New Relationships

Friends are the family we choose, and their significance in our lives cannot be overstated. As you navigate the waters of a new romantic relationship, remember that your friends need to feel valued too.

- **Maintain Traditions**: If you have standing traditions with your friends, such as weekly dinners or movie nights, strive to keep them alive. These rituals are important touchstones in your friendships.

- **Be Present**: When spending time with friends, be fully present. Avoid constantly checking your phone or talking excessively about your new partner. Your friends deserve your undivided attention.

- **Support Their Lives** : Show interest and support for your friends' activities and relationships. Reciprocity is key in any relationship, and your friends will appreciate your enthusiasm for their lives.

Extended Family Ties: Integrating New Partners with Grace

Extended family can play a significant role in our support systems, and it's important to consider their feelings as you introduce a new partner into the fold.

- **Ease Into Introductions**: Gradually introduce your partner to extended family members. Start with smaller gatherings before moving on to larger family events. This gives everyone time to adjust and get to know each other.

- **Respect Traditions**: Be mindful of family traditions and how your new relationship might impact them. Work together with your partner and family to find the best way to honor these customs.

- **Encourage Connections**: Encourage your partner to build their own relationships with your extended family. This can help them feel more integrated and accepted.

The New Intimate Relationship: Fostering a Supportive Network

Your new intimate relationship should be a source of joy and growth, not stress and division among your loved ones. By fostering a supportive network, you can ensure that all your relationships thrive.

- **Set Boundaries**: Establish boundaries with your partner regarding time spent with family and friends. This ensures that no one feels neglected and that your relationship remains healthy.

- **Communicate Needs**: Share your needs and expectations with your partner, and encourage them to do the same. Understanding each other's social needs can help prevent conflicts.

- **Build a Community**: Aim to build a community that includes your partner, siblings, friends, and extended family. Group activities and shared experiences can strengthen the bonds between everyone involved.

The Harmony of Love's Many Forms

Love is not a finite resource, but it does require thoughtful distribution. By consciously balancing the affection we show to siblings, friends, and extended family, we can nurture all our relationships, even as we explore new romantic ones. Remember, the conservation of love is not about dividing your heart but about expanding it to embrace all the meaningful connections in your life. With empathy, communication, and a little planning, you can maintain the harmony of love's many forms.

The Role of Cultural Expectations in Shaping Love

Love, an emotion as old as humanity itself, is universally experienced yet diversely expressed. The tapestry of human affection is colored by the myriad cultural norms that dictate its distribution and manifestation within personal relationships. This exploration delves into the intricate ways in which cultural expectations shape the way we give and receive love, and the profound impact these norms can have on our intimate connections.

Understanding Cultural Norms and Love

Cultural norms act as invisible guides, steering the course of our emotional expressions and interpersonal dynamics. These unwritten rules are passed down through generations, subtly influencing our understanding of love and how it should be displayed. From grand romantic gestures to the quiet, steadfast support, the spectrum of love's expression is as varied as the cultures that celebrate it. Recognizing these differences is key to appreciating the full range of human affection and the richness it brings to our lives.

Love's Many Languages

The concept of love languages, popularized by Dr. Gary Chapman, highlights the importance of understanding individual preferences in expressing and receiving love. These preferences are often rooted in cultural backgrounds, shaping expectations and interpretations of affection. Whether it's through words of affirmation, acts of service, receiving gifts, quality time, or physical touch, each culture places a different emphasis on these languages, creating a unique blueprint for love's expression.

Navigating Cross-Cultural Relationships

In our increasingly interconnected world, cross-cultural relationships are becoming more common, bringing together individuals with distinct views on love and affection. Navigating these differences requires patience, empathy, and open communication. By embracing the diversity of cultural expectations, couples can forge a harmonious blend of traditions and create a shared language of love that honours both of their backgrounds.

The Impact on Personal Relationships

Cultural expectations can both enrich and challenge personal relationships. When aligned, they provide a sense of unity and understanding. However, when expectations clash, they can lead to misunderstandings and conflict. It is essential for individuals to engage in self-reflection and dialogue, striving to bridge the gap between differing cultural norms. In doing so, they can foster deeper connections and a more profound appreciation for the diverse ways in which love can be expressed.

Cultural norms are powerful forces that shape the way love is distributed and expressed in personal relationships. By exploring and understanding these cultural expectations, we can enhance our emotional connections and celebrate the rich diversity of love's expressions. Embracing this complexity not only strengthens our relationships but also enriches our lives with a deeper understanding of the human heart.

Navigating the Shifts in Love: Embracing Change with an Open Heart

Love is an ever-evolving journey, a dance that moves to the rhythm of life's changes. As we traverse through different stages of life, the dynamics of our relationships inevitably shift, bringing forth new challenges and opportunities for growth. Understanding and embracing these changes can lead to a deeper, more resilient love that endures through the ebbs and flows of life.

Understanding the Emotional Landscape

The emotional landscape of love is rich and varied, marked by peaks of joy and valleys of sorrow. As we encounter life's milestones—whether it's a new addition to the family, the empty nest syndrome, or the natural progression of a romantic relationship—our emotional responses can be as diverse as the experiences themselves. It's important to recognize that these shifts are not only natural but also necessary for the evolution of our relationships.

-**Embrace the change**: Acknowledge that change is a constant and that your feelings will adapt over time. Celebrate the new chapters in your life and the unique ways in which love manifests during these periods.

-**Communicate openly**: Share your feelings with your loved ones. Open communication fosters understanding and helps prevent misunderstandings during times of change.

-**Seek support**: Don't hesitate to reach out to friends, family, or professionals for guidance and support as you navigate new emotional terrains.

Balancing Love in a Shifting Family Dynamic

As families grow and change, so too does the distribution of our time, attention, and affection. It's crucial to maintain a balance of love among all relationships, ensuring that no one feels neglected or overshadowed by the changes.

-**Prioritize quality time**: Make an effort to spend quality time with each family member. It's not just about the quantity of time but the quality of the interactions that strengthens bonds.

-**Foster individual relationships**: While family time is important, nurturing individual relationships within the family is equally vital. This helps each member feel valued and understood on a personal level.

-**Adapt to new roles**: Be open to the new roles you and your family members may take on. Whether it's becoming a parent, a grandparent, or a partner, each role comes with its own set of responsibilities and joys.

Cultivating Resilience in Love

Resilience in love means having the strength to withstand life's storms and the flexibility to adapt to new circumstances. It's about building a foundation of trust, respect, and mutual support that can weather any change.

-**Practice empathy**: Put yourself in your loved ones' shoes. Understanding their perspective can help you respond with compassion and empathy during times of change.

-**Celebrate growth**: Recognize that each shift in your relationship is an opportunity for growth. Celebrate the milestones and the lessons learned along the way.

-**Stay committed**: Reaffirm your commitment to your loved ones regularly. A strong commitment can serve as an anchor during turbulent times.

Nurturing Love Through Life's Seasons

Just as the seasons change, so do the seasons of love. Each phase brings its own beauty and challenges, and learning to appreciate the present moment is key to nurturing love.

-**Appreciate the now**: Savor the current stage of your relationship. Whether it's the excitement of new love or the comfort of a long-standing bond, there is beauty to be found in every season.

-**Plan for the future**: While living in the moment is important, it's also wise to plan for the future. Discuss your hopes and dreams with your loved ones, and work together to make them a reality.

-**Reflect on the past**: Look back on your journey with gratitude. Reflecting on the past can provide valuable insights and strengthen your appreciation for the love you share.

Love's Enduring Promise

Navigating the shifts in love is a journey that requires patience, understanding, and a willingness to adapt. By embracing change with an open heart, communicating effectively, and nurturing our relationships through every season, we can maintain a balance of love that stands the test of time. Remember, the conservation of love is not about keeping things the same; it's about allowing love to grow and evolve, just as we do. With awareness and effort, we can ensure that love remains a constant source of strength and joy in our lives, no matter what changes come our way.

Emotional Intelligence: The Key to Sharing Love Generously

Emotional intelligence (EI) is the silent conductor orchestrating the symphony of our interpersonal relationships. It is the ability to perceive, understand, and manage not only our own emotions but also those of others. When it comes to love—a profound and complex emotion—emotional intelligence becomes the cornerstone for its effective distribution. In this exploration, we delve into the ways EI enhances our capacity to share love, fostering deeper connections and nurturing the bonds that hold us together.

Understanding Emotional Intelligence in the Realm of Love

At its core, emotional intelligence is about awareness. It's the recognition of the fact that love is not a finite resource but a renewable energy that thrives on being shared. However, to distribute love effectively, one must first be adept at decoding the emotional landscapes within themselves and others. This means being attuned to the subtle cues of affection, the silent pleas for attention, and the unspoken words that yearn for understanding. By cultivating a keen sense of emotional awareness, we become better equipped to give love in the ways that truly resonate with those we care about.

The Art of Managing Emotions for Harmonious Relationships

Managing emotions is akin to navigating a vast ocean; it requires skill, patience, and a deep understanding of the currents that drive our feelings. In the context of love, this involves tempering our reactions, showing empathy, and exercising patience. Emotional intelligence teaches us that love is not just about grand gestures but also about the small acts of kindness that accumulate over time. It's about knowing when to offer a shoulder to lean on, when to give space, and when to engage in meaningful dialogue. By mastering our emotional responses, we create an environment where love can flourish unimpeded.

Empathy: The Bridge to Authentic Connections

Empathy is the heartbeat of emotional intelligence. It allows us to step into the shoes of another, to feel their joy and their pain, and to extend love in a way that is both genuine and healing. Empathy goes beyond mere sympathy; it is an active engagement with the emotional experiences of others. When we empathize, we build bridges of understanding that can withstand the weight of conflict and the erosion of time. In doing so, we ensure that the love we share is not just received but also felt at the deepest levels of connection.

The Ripple Effect of Emotional Intelligence in Love Distribution

The beauty of emotional intelligence lies in its ripple effect. When we share love with emotional intelligence, we not only enrich our own lives but also inspire others to do the same. This creates a virtuous cycle of love that expands outward, touching the lives of friends, family, and even strangers. Emotional intelligence encourages us to be mindful of the impact our words and actions have on the emotional well-being of others. It reminds us that love, when given freely and with understanding, has the power to transform the world around us—one heart at a time.

Cultivating Emotional Intelligence for a Lifetime of Love

Developing emotional intelligence is a lifelong journey. It requires introspection, practice, and a willingness to learn from our interactions. The good news is that EI can be nurtured and grown, much like a garden of love. By committing to self-improvement, seeking feedback, and engaging in active listening, we can enhance our ability to share love in the most meaningful ways. Remember, the distribution of love is not just about the quantity but the quality of our emotional connections. Let us strive to be emotionally intelligent lovers, friends, and companions, for it is through this wisdom that we can truly make the world a more loving place.

Emotional intelligence is not just a tool for personal development; it is the essence of how we connect, share, and thrive in our relationships. By embracing the principles of EI, we can ensure that the love we distribute is not only abundant but also transformative. Let us continue to learn, grow, and love with emotional intelligence as our guide.

The Ripple Effect of Love: A Journey Through the Waves of Our Relationships

Love, in its purest form, is akin to a pebble tossed into the vast ocean of human experience. It creates ripples that extend far beyond the initial splash, touching lives and reshaping destinies in ways we can scarcely imagine. This profound influence of love within our personal relationships is not just a fleeting moment of affection but a powerful force that can elevate our well-being and bring harmony to our social networks.

The Power of Love in Personal Growth

When we think of love, we often envision romantic partnerships or familial bonds. However, the scope of love's impact is much broader, encompassing friendships, mentorships, and even brief encounters with strangers. Each act of kindness, each word of encouragement, and each gesture of support sends out ripples that contribute to our personal growth. As we navigate through life's challenges, the love we give and receive becomes a beacon of hope, guiding us towards resilience and self-discovery.

Love's Influence on Interpersonal Connections

The beauty of love's ripple effect is most evident in the way it strengthens our connections with others. A single act of compassion can inspire others to pay it forward, creating a chain reaction of goodwill. This interconnectedness not only fosters a sense of belonging but also cultivates an environment where trust and cooperation flourish. In a world where individualism often takes precedence, the distribution of love reminds us of the value of community and the strength found in unity.

Cultivating Harmony in Our Social Networks

The ripples of love extend beyond our immediate circle, influencing the broader social fabric in which we exist. When we approach our interactions with empathy and understanding, we contribute to a culture of acceptance and peace. This harmonious atmosphere not only benefits our own social circles but also sets a precedent for societal norms. By prioritizing love in our daily lives, we can play a part in creating a more compassionate and inclusive world.

Reflections on the Enduring Impact of Love

As we reflect on the ripple effect of love, it becomes clear that its true power lies in its enduring impact. The love we share today can echo through generations, shaping the lives of those we may never meet. It is a testament to the timeless nature of love and its capacity to transcend barriers. By embracing love in all its forms, we leave a legacy of kindness that will continue to resonate long after we are gone.

The ripple effect of love is a testament to the transformative power of our most cherished emotion. It is a reminder that every interaction, every moment of connection, has the potential to alter the course of our lives and those around us. As we journey through the waves of our relationships, let us be mindful of the ripples we create and the legacy of love we leave in our wake.

Chapter 3: Love and Marriage

We delve into the intricate dance between love and marriage, exploring the ways in which these two profound elements of human experience intertwine. We'll uncover the subtle shifts in the heart's economy as partners navigate the ebb and flow of emotional investment within the sacred bond of matrimony.

Marriage, often seen as the harbor of love, is more than a simple merger of lives; it's a dynamic journey of growth and adaptation. As we peel back the layers, we'll discover how love matures and transforms in the crucible of lifelong commitment, and how couples find new depths of affection and understanding through shared experiences.

We'll also consider the challenges that couples face, acknowledging that the path of marriage is not always smooth. The resilience of love in the face of life's storms is a testament to the strength that can be forged within the partnership. .

Furthermore, we'll celebrate the diversity of love and marriage across cultures, recognizing that while the expression of love may vary widely, its essence remains a universal language. This exploration will enrich our appreciation for the myriad ways in which love is woven into the fabric of marriage around the world.

Embracing Change: Welcoming a New Partner into Your Life

Understanding the Emotional Shift

When we open our hearts to a new partner, it's akin to rearranging the furniture of our emotional landscape. This isn't just about finding more love; it's about redistributing the love we already have in a way that accommodates this significant new presence. Imagine your heart as a garden where love blossoms for family and friends. Now, envision a new, vibrant flower blooming—this is the love for your partner. It's not that the garden gets bigger; rather, we tend to the new flower, ensuring it has enough space, nutrients, and sunlight. This might mean that some of the other flowers get a little less attention, but the overall beauty of the garden remains.

The Balancing Act

Consider the delicate balance of your relationships as a pie chart of emotional investment. Before, your family might have been the largest slice, with friends taking up the remainder. Now, a new slice appears for your spouse, and it's a substantial one. This doesn't mean the love for family and friends diminishes; it's simply that the pie has been divided differently. You might find yourself allocating 50% of your emotional energy to your spouse, 35% to family, and 15% to friends. It's a new equilibrium, one that reflects the importance of your partner while still honoring the existing bonds in your life.

Navigating the Transition

Adjusting to this new dynamic can be challenging. It's like learning a new dance with your loved ones, where everyone is trying to find their rhythm. Communication is key. Talk to your family and friends about the changes. More importantly, listen to their feelings and reassure them that they are still valued. It's about finding a new normal where everyone feels secure and loved. Remember, it's not about giving less to some but about sharing your love in a way that enriches all your relationships.

The Ripple Effect of New Love

The introduction of a spouse into your life doesn't just affect your time and emotions; it influences your priorities, decisions, and future plans. This ripple effect can be profound, but it's also a testament to the power of love. It's important to embrace this change with an open heart and mind. Recognize that this shift is not just about accommodating another person but about growing and evolving as an individual and as part of a couple. Your new partner brings their own garden of love, and together, you'll cultivate a landscape that's rich, diverse, and ever-flourishing.

Maintaining Harmony in Your Emotional Ecosystem

As you navigate this new chapter, strive for balance and harmony in your emotional ecosystem. It's okay to reassess and reallocate your emotional investments from time to time. Life is dynamic, and so are relationships. The key is to nurture all your connections with intention and care. By doing so, you'll find that the love you give not only multiplies but also creates a more vibrant and fulfilling life for you and all those you hold dear.

Remember, the entry of a new significant other is not just about sharing your love; it's about expanding it in ways that can bring joy and fulfillment to every corner of your emotional garden.

Reallocating Love: Adjustments and Equilibrium

Marriage is a beautiful journey that begins with a promise of eternal companionship, but it also brings about a significant shift in life's dynamics. The art of finding equilibrium after tying the knot is akin to a delicate dance of give and take. It's about discovering a harmonious balance between the love you share with your partner and the love you have for the other important people in your life, such as your parents, friends, and even yourself.

The Dance of Compromise

Imagine a dance floor where each person represents a different aspect of your life. Your partner is your dance partner, moving in step with you, but around you are other dancers – your family, friends, and career. Initially, you might step on each other's toes as you learn to move together. A newlywed might find themselves torn between spending a quiet evening with their spouse and attending a family gathering. It's a common scenario that requires patience and understanding. Over time, you learn to glide across the dance floor, striking a balance that allows you to spend quality time with your partner while also honoring commitments to family and friends.

The Language of Love

Communication is the bedrock of any successful relationship, and it becomes even more crucial when you're navigating the waters of post-marriage adjustments. It's important to express your needs and listen to your partner's expectations. For instance, discussing how to spend holidays or allocate time for date nights can prevent feelings of neglect or frustration. By using "I feel" statements rather than accusatory "You never" remarks, you foster a safe space for open dialogue. This way, both partners feel heard and respected, paving the way for a balanced relationship that accommodates the needs of both individuals.

The Symphony of Support

Support systems are invaluable, and it's essential to recognize that seeking help is not a sign of weakness but of strength. Sometimes, finding equilibrium means leaning on friends for advice or engaging in couple's therapy to navigate through rough patches. It's about building a network that uplifts and supports your union. For example, a friend might offer to host a dinner so you can have a night off from family obligations, or a therapist might provide tools to better manage your time and expectations. Embrace the support around you, and you'll find that the journey to equilibrium becomes a shared experience rather than a solitary struggle.

The Seasons of Change

As with the changing seasons, life after marriage will ebb and flow. There will be periods of effortless harmony and times when the scales tip, demanding more attention on one side. Perhaps a job change requires more of your time, or a family member needs extra care. These fluctuations are natural, and the key is to adapt and recalibrate. Keep the lines of communication open, and be willing to reassess and make new adjustments as your circumstances evolve. Remember, the goal is not to achieve a perfect balance at all times but to navigate the changes together, hand in hand.

The Journey Ahead

Ultimately, the journey to finding equilibrium in your marriage is ongoing and ever-changing. It's about embracing the process of adjustment and compromise, celebrating the small victories, and learning from the challenges. As you and your partner grow together, you'll discover that the rhythm you create is unique to your relationship. It's a dance that belongs only to the two of you, choreographed by the love and respect you share. So take each step with intention, support each other through the missteps, and cherish the beautiful balance you build together, day by day.

In the dance of marriage, adjustments and equilibrium are the steps that lead to a lifetime of harmony. Keep dancing, keep communicating, and let love guide you to your perfect balance.

Case Studies: Love Redistribution in Marriages Across Cultures

Understanding how love is expressed and prioritized in marriages across different cultures can be a fascinating study in human relationships. The concept of "love redistribution" refers to the way love is shared and expressed within a marriage and extended to family members. Cultural backgrounds play a pivotal role in shaping these dynamics, often reflecting broader societal values and norms.

The Influence of Culture on Marital Love

In many collectivist societies, where the group's needs are often placed above the individual's, love is seen as a resource that is not exclusively reserved for the marital relationship. Instead, it is distributed among a wider circle of family members, including parents, siblings, and even extended relatives. This communal approach to love emphasizes the importance of maintaining strong family bonds and supporting one another, often at the expense of the exclusivity of the marital relationship.

Individualism vs. Collectivism

Contrastingly, in individualistic cultures, where personal autonomy and self-fulfillment are highly valued, the spouse often becomes the primary recipient of one's love and emotional energy. This can lead to a more intense and exclusive marital bond, with less emphasis on the extended family. The expectation is that the couple will prioritize each other above all else, which can sometimes lead to a more insular family unit.

Case Study Examples

For instance, in a typical Indian marriage, which reflects a collectivist culture, it's common for newlyweds to live with the groom's parents. Love and care are shared among all members of the household, and the couple's relationship is integrated into the larger family dynamic. On the other hand, in the United States, which exemplifies an individualistic culture, newlyweds are more likely to set up their own independent household, focusing on building a life together separate from their parents and other relatives.

Balancing Love in a Globalized World

As the world becomes more interconnected, these cultural norms are increasingly coming into contact and sometimes conflict. Couples from different cultural backgrounds may have to navigate and negotiate how to redistribute love in their marriage, striving to honor their cultural heritage while also building a relationship that works for them as individuals. This can be a delicate balance to achieve, but it also offers an opportunity for growth and a deeper understanding of each other's values and expectations.

The redistribution of love in marriages across cultures is a complex and nuanced phenomenon that reflects deeper societal values and individual expectations. Whether in collectivist or individualistic societies, couples must work together to find a balance that honors their cultural backgrounds while fostering a strong, healthy marital relationship. As we continue to explore and understand these dynamics, we gain valuable insights into the universal nature of love and the diverse ways it can be expressed and shared within the tapestry of human relationships.

The Role of Communication in Rebalancing Love

Love, as we know, is the cornerstone of any marriage. It's the spark that ignites the union of two souls and the glue that holds them together through the ups and downs of life. However, as time passes, the scales of affection can sometimes tip, leading to a need for rebalancing. This is where the power of communication comes into play, acting as a pivotal tool in restoring equilibrium within the relationship.

The Essence of Open Dialogue

Takeaway: Open communication is the lifeblood of a thriving marriage, especially when it comes to recalibrating the love shared between partners.

Imagine a garden that represents your marriage. Just as plants need water to grow, your relationship needs the nourishment of open dialogue to flourish. Couples must create a safe space where they can freely express their needs, desires, and concerns without fear of judgment. This means actively listening to each other and validating feelings, which fosters a deeper understanding and connection. For instance, setting aside a dedicated "us time" each week can be a simple yet effective way for partners to reconnect and ensure that both feel heard and cherished.

Navigating the Challenges Together

Example:A couple might set aside time to discuss how they can ensure their parents still feel loved and valued after their marriage.

Life is a mosaic of moments—some joyous, others challenging. When faced with obstacles, it's crucial for couples to navigate them together through open communication. Whether it's discussing how to maintain strong relationships with extended family or tackling financial hurdles, approaching these conversations with empathy and a team mindset strengthens the bond between partners. By sharing the load and working towards solutions together, couples can reinforce their commitment to each other and the love they share.

The Art of Compromise

Compromise is an art that requires both partners to give and take with grace. Through honest communication, couples can identify areas where they're willing to bend to accommodate each other's needs. This doesn't mean sacrificing one's happiness for the other, but rather finding a middle ground where both partners feel their love is balanced and respected. It's about crafting a partnership where both individuals can thrive, both as a couple and as individuals.

Celebrating Each Other's Growth

As individuals evolve, so does the nature of their love. Open communication allows couples to celebrate each other's personal growth and the positive impact it has on their relationship. Acknowledging and supporting each other's dreams and aspirations can rekindle the passion and admiration that may have dimmed over time. It's a beautiful cycle: as each person grows, the relationship does too, leading to a more profound and resilient love.

The Continuous Journey of Love

Communication is not just a tool but a journey that couples embark on together—a journey of constant learning, understanding, and rebalancing. It's about building a bridge between hearts, where words are the stones that strengthen the connection. Remember, the goal isn't to avoid imbalances in love but to navigate them with grace and mutual respect. By committing to open and honest communication, couples can ensure that their love not only endures but thrives in the ever-changing landscape of life.

Maintaining Individuality Within Marriage

Marriage is a beautiful journey of partnership, where two individuals come together to share their lives. However, it's crucial to remember that being part of a duo doesn't mean losing one's sense of self. In fact, nurturing individuality can lead to a healthier and more fulfilling relationship. Here are some insights on how to maintain your personal identity while growing together as a couple.

Embrace Personal Interests and Hobbies

It's essential to have activities that you love doing on your own. Whether it's a sport, an art form, or a hobby, these personal interests are a reflection of who you are. For instance, a husband might spend Saturday mornings on the basketball court with his friends, while his wife might relish the lively discussions at her monthly book club. These activities not only provide a sense of accomplishment and joy but also bring new experiences and ideas into the marriage, enriching conversations and mutual understanding.

Set Aside Time for Yourself

In the midst of shared responsibilities and routines, it's important to carve out time for yourself. This could be as simple as enjoying a quiet morning coffee alone, taking a solo walk, or indulging in a long bath. This "me time" allows you to recharge, reflect, and maintain a sense of independence. It's not about being apart from your spouse, but about giving yourself the space to grow and thrive individually, which in turn, benefits the relationship.

Support Each Other's Goals and Dreams

A supportive partner is a gift in any marriage. Encouraging each other's aspirations is a way of showing respect for your spouse's individuality. Whether it's pursuing further education, starting a business, or training for a marathon, being each other's cheerleader fosters a deep bond of trust and admiration. It's about celebrating each other's successes and being there during the challenges, knowing that each person's achievements contribute to the strength of the union.

Communicate Openly and Honestly

Open communication is the cornerstone of any healthy relationship. It's important to discuss your need for individuality with your spouse. Share your thoughts on why personal space is important to you and how it can positively impact your marriage. Listen to your partner's perspective and find a balance that works for both of you. Remember, it's not about keeping secrets but about maintaining a sense of self within the shared life you've built together.

Respect Boundaries and Differences

Every individual has their own set of boundaries and it's important to respect them. This could mean understanding when your partner needs time alone or recognizing that you have different ways of handling stress. It's also about appreciating the differences in interests and opinions that make each of you unique. By honoring these boundaries, you create a marriage where both partners feel valued for who they are, not just for the role they play in the relationship.

The Impact of Children on Love's Distribution

The arrival of children into a family is a transformative event that reshapes the emotional landscape in profound ways. It's a time of joy, wonder, and, inevitably, adjustment, as parents navigate the complexities of balancing their love and attention. The dynamic of love within a family is not a zero-sum game, but rather a fluid and evolving exchange that requires care and mindfulness to maintain harmony and connection.

A New Focus of Affection

When a child enters the picture, it's as if a new gravitational force emerges, pulling the hearts of parents into a fresh orbit. This tiny being, with their immediate and pressing needs, becomes a central focus of affection and concern. Parents often find themselves instinctively prioritizing their child, ensuring that this new life is nurtured and cherished. This shift is natural and necessary, but it also calls for a delicate balancing act to ensure that other relationships, particularly the marital bond, continue to thrive.

Maintaining the Marital Bond

The marital relationship, which may have once been the sole recipient of romantic love and attention, now shares the stage with a new and demanding presence. It's crucial for partners to consciously carve out time for each other, to continue nurturing their connection amidst the whirlwind of parenting. This might mean scheduling regular date nights, finding moments for affection, or simply communicating openly about each other's needs and feelings. By doing so, parents can demonstrate that while the distribution of love has expanded, the depth of their commitment to one another remains steadfast.

Love Grows and Multiplies

It's a common misconception that love is a finite resource that diminishes as it's divided among more people. In reality, the heart's capacity for love is not fixed; it grows and stretches with each new relationship. The addition of a child can amplify the love within a family, creating new dimensions of affection and care that enrich everyone involved. As parents, siblings, and extended family members bond with the child, the network of love becomes more intricate and robust.

Embracing the Journey Together

Ultimately, the impact of children on love's distribution is a journey of continuous learning and adaptation. It's about embracing the changes, celebrating the expansion of love, and supporting one another through the challenges. As families grow and evolve, so too does the love that binds them, becoming a dynamic and inclusive force that has the power to transform every member for the better. By acknowledging the complexities and approaching them with intention and grace, families can ensure that love's distribution is not only preserved but is also allowed to flourish in new and beautiful ways.

The Dynamic Journey of Marital Love

Marital love is akin to a river that flows through the landscape of life, constantly adapting to the contours of experiences and time. It's a profound connection that refuses to remain stagnant, instead choosing to evolve with each shared triumph and tribulation. As couples embark on this journey together, they discover that the essence of their love is not fixed but is an ever-changing tapestry woven from the threads of their shared experiences.

Deepening Bonds Over Time

As the years pass, the initial flames of passion that often characterize the early stages of marriage may give way to a more profound and nuanced form of love. This mature love is characterized by a deep understanding and acceptance of one another. It's not uncommon for couples to find that, as they grow older, their love deepens, becoming richer and more complex. This evolution is a testament to the resilience and adaptability of marital love, as it becomes less about idealization and more about genuine connection and companionship.

Navigating Life's Challenges Together

Life inevitably presents a myriad of challenges, from career changes and health issues to the complexities of raising a family. Each obstacle offers an opportunity for marital love to adapt and grow stronger. Couples learn to lean on each other, developing a partnership that is capable of withstanding life's storms. Through these shared experiences, partners often find that their love becomes more inclusive, taking into account not just their own needs but also the well-being of their spouse.

Balancing Relationships with Others

As individuals, we are not islands, and our marital relationships exist within a broader social context. Over time, couples become more adept at balancing their love for each other with their relationships with friends, family, and the community. This balance is crucial, as it allows for a healthy interdependence where both partners can thrive both within and outside the marriage. It's a delicate dance that, when mastered, can lead to a more fulfilling and harmonious life together.

Embracing Change as a Constant

The only constant in life is change, and this is especially true for marital love. Embracing this fact allows couples to remain flexible and open to the evolution of their relationship. Whether it's adapting to each other's personal growth or the inevitable shifts in life circumstances, the ability to navigate change together is a hallmark of a strong and enduring marital bond.

Reflections on Love's Fluidity

Love, in its essence, is a remarkable force, ever-changing and evolving with the passage of time and the unfolding of life's myriad events. It is not a static emotion, confined to a single shape or expression, but rather a dynamic and adaptable presence in our lives. This fluidity of love allows it to endure through the seasons of our existence, transforming itself to meet the needs of the moment and the individuals involved.

The Transformative Power of Love

Consider the journey of a long-term relationship, where love's initial spark—a fiery, passionate blaze—gradually evolves into a warm, glowing ember of deep companionship and mutual respect. This transformation is not a diminishment but an expansion of love's capacity to nurture and sustain. It is a testament to love's inherent flexibility that it can morph from the heady rush of new romance into the quiet strength of a shared life.

Love's Many Forms

Love's fluidity is also evident in the way it can manifest in different forms. There is the fierce, protective love of a parent for a child, the platonic yet profound bond between friends, and the tender, nurturing care we can show for ourselves. Each of these expressions of love is unique, yet they all spring from the same well of human emotion, demonstrating love's versatility and its ability to touch every aspect of our lives.

Adapting to Life's Changes

Life is a series of changes—some anticipated, others unexpected. Love's fluid nature equips us to adapt to these changes, reshaping our relationships as necessary. A couple may find that the birth of a child, a career change, or the challenges of aging require them to reinvent their love, discovering new depths and dimensions they hadn't explored before. Love's resilience lies in its ability to bend without breaking, to adjust without losing its core essence.

Embracing Love's Journey

As we reflect on love's fluidity, we come to appreciate the beauty of its journey. It is a voyage that takes us through calm seas and turbulent waves, always moving, always flowing. By embracing the fluid nature of love, we open ourselves to the full spectrum of its experiences, learning to ride its tides with grace and gratitude. Love, in all its forms, remains one of life's most profound mysteries and its most precious gifts.

Chapter 4: The Intriguing Equations of Affection

We delve into the fascinating world where numbers and emotions intertwine. "The Mathematics of Love" is more than just a poetic concept; it's a realm where the heart's complexities are translated into the universal language of mathematics. By employing models and equations, we gain a unique perspective on the dynamics of love, allowing us to chart its ebbs and flows with surprising clarity. Whether it's the initial spark or the enduring flame, mathematics offers a novel lens through which to examine the patterns of passion.

As we navigate through the intricate dance of attraction and attachment, we discover that love, much like any other natural phenomenon, can be quantified and perhaps even predicted. This chapter isn't just for the mathematically inclined; it's a journey for anyone who's ever been curious about the forces that govern our closest connections. Through engaging examples and accessible explanations, we'll see how the distribution of love can shift over time, providing insights that might just help us understand the heart's most mysterious workings.

Modelling Love Using Mathematical Principles

Love, an emotion as old as humanity itself, has been the subject of countless poems, songs, and stories. But can something as complex and profound as love be quantified and modeled using the language of mathematics? The answer is a resounding yes.

Mathematical models can indeed represent the intricacies of love's distribution and dynamics, offering a unique perspective on how we allocate our affection among the significant relationships in our lives.

The Equation of Love

Imagine love as a resource that we choose to distribute among our family, friends, and romantic partners. This distribution can be represented by a system of linear equations, where each variable corresponds to the percentage of love dedicated to each relationship. For instance, let `L_f` represent love for family, `L_fr` for friends, and `L_p` for a partner. We can then create equations that reflect the balance we strive to maintain:

$$L\_f + L\_fr + L\_p = 100\%$$

This simple equation ensures that the total love distributed does not exceed our emotional capacity, symbolized by 100%.

Balancing the Love Ledger

But how do we decide the right balance? That's where the complexity of human emotions comes into play. Each person's life circumstances, values, and experiences shape their unique love ledger. A new parent might allocate a larger percentage to `L_f`, while a young adult might prioritize `L_fr` as they navigate the world with their peers. The beauty of this model is its flexibility; it can adapt to the changing tides of our lives.

The Dynamics of Love

The dynamics of love are not static. They are influenced by time, events, and our interactions with others. To capture this, we can introduce variables that change over time, such as `t` for time, and functions that describe how love grows or fades:

$$L\_f(t) = a * t + b$$

$$L\_fr(t) = c * t^2 + d$$

$$L\_p(t) = e * t^3 + f$$

These functions suggest that love for family might increase linearly with time, while love for friends could grow at a faster rate, and romantic love might have an even more complex pattern.

The Limits of Love

It's important to recognize that our capacity for love is not infinite. Constraints in our model can represent the limits of time, energy, and emotional bandwidth. For example, if we dedicate more time to our partner, we might have less time for friends, and this trade-off can be represented by inequalities:

$$L\_f + L\_fr \leq 70\%$$

$$L\_p \leq 50\%$$

These constraints ensure that we do not overcommit ourselves, preserving our emotional well-being.

Love in the Real World

While mathematical models provide a structured way to think about love, they cannot capture its full essence. Love is more than numbers and equations; it's about the quality of our connections and the depth of our feelings. However, by using these models, we can gain insights into our emotional priorities and make more informed decisions about how we allocate our most precious resource: our love.

Modelling love using mathematical principles offers a fascinating glimpse into the rational aspects of our emotional lives. It helps us understand the balance and dynamics of our relationships in a quantifiable way. While love will always remain a profoundly human experience, mathematics can provide a valuable framework for reflecting on the choices we make in our hearts.

Graphs and Functions: Visualizing Love Distribution

Love, an emotion as old as humanity itself, is often felt but not easily quantified. Yet, in our quest to understand the dynamics of our relationships, we turn to the visual power of graphs and functions. These tools allow us to map out the intricate web of affections and commitments that make up our personal worlds. By doing so, we gain a unique perspective on how love is distributed across our lives and how it evolves with the tides of time and circumstance.

The Power of Pie: A Slice of Emotional Insight

Imagine a pie chart, its colorful segments representing the various loves in your life: family, friends, partners, even pets. Each slice is a visual testament to the time and energy you invest in these relationships. But what happens when life throws us a curveball? Significant events, such as tying the knot or welcoming a new family member, can dramatically alter this pie of affection.

Before and After: The Love Shift

Before a major event, your pie chart might show a relatively balanced distribution of love. Friends and hobbies might take up substantial portions, with family and romantic relationships claiming their fair shares. However, after an event like marriage, the chart morphs. The slice for your spouse becomes more substantial, symbolizing the deepening bond and increased commitment. Similarly, the birth of a child introduces a new slice, one that grows steadily as this new life becomes central to your heart.

The Love Line: Tracking Emotional Investment Over Time

Beyond pie charts, line graphs offer another perspective. They trace the ebb and flow of our emotional investments over time, revealing patterns and trends. For instance, the line representing love for a partner might show a steady climb, punctuated by spikes during anniversaries and shared triumphs. Conversely, it might dip during periods of conflict or distance, only to recover as issues are resolved and intimacy is rekindled.

The Balancing Act: Juggling Life's Loves

As we navigate life's journey, our love line graph becomes a complex dance of rises and falls. The arrival of a child might temporarily lower the attention given to hobbies, as depicted by a descending line. Yet, over time, we strive to rebalance our graph, ensuring that no part of our life lacks the love it deserves. This visual tool empowers us to consciously adjust our time and energy, maintaining harmony in our personal universe.

The Heart's Geography: Mapping Love's Landscape

Another fascinating approach is the use of topographical maps to represent the landscape of our affections. Peaks symbolize the high points of our relationships, while valleys might indicate periods of emotional distance or neglect. By examining the contours of our heart's geography, we can identify which relationships need nurturing to reach new heights and which ones are thriving on love's summit.

Embracing the Visual Journey

Graphs and functions are not just mathematical constructs; they are mirrors reflecting the depth and breadth of our emotional lives. By visualizing love distribution, we gain insights into the health and balance of our relationships. We can celebrate the areas where love abounds and address the parts that may need more care. In the end, these visualizations are not just about understanding love; they're about actively shaping it, ensuring that every slice of our pie, every point on our line, and every peak on our map is as full of love as it can be.

In the grand scheme of things, love may be immeasurable, but through the lens of graphs and functions, we can see its shape and form. We can adjust, nurture, and grow our capacity for love, making sure that every relationship in our life is as rich and fulfilling as possible. So, the next time you ponder the state of your heart, consider plotting a graph or two—it might just reveal the path to a more balanced and love-filled life.

Predictive Analysis: Navigating the Tides of Heartfelt Connections

In the intricate dance of human relationships, love remains an enigmatic force, shaping our lives in profound ways. As we journey through the ebbs and flows of connection and affection, the concept of predictive analysis emerges as a beacon, offering insights into the future of our most cherished bonds. By harnessing the power of data and patterns, we can begin to forecast the subtle shifts in the dynamics of love, anticipating how new relationships or significant life events might influence the distribution of our emotional investments.

The Heart's Compass: Steering Through New Relationships

Imagine embarking on a new relationship, the excitement and uncertainty mingling in a whirlwind of emotions. Here, predictive models serve as a compass, guiding us through uncharted waters. By analyzing past behaviors and outcomes, these models can provide a glimpse into how a new partnership might evolve, helping individuals and couples navigate the complexities of their burgeoning love with greater confidence and understanding.

The Ripple Effect of Life's Milestones

Life's milestones, such as the arrival of a child, can send ripples through the pond of our existing relationships, altering the distribution of love and attention. A predictive model, meticulously crafted to consider various factors such as time, energy, and emotional bandwidth, can estimate the impact of such an event. It can offer a roadmap for couples and families, enabling them to balance their love and ensure that each member feels valued and supported during these transformative times.

Embracing Change with Open Arms

Change is an inevitable companion on the journey of love, and embracing it with open arms can lead to a deeper and more resilient connection. Predictive analysis does not claim to have all the answers, but it provides a framework for understanding potential outcomes. By considering the insights offered by these models, individuals can prepare for the changes ahead, fostering a flexible and adaptive approach to their relationships.

The Symphony of Extended Connections

When we consider love, it's not just the romantic bond between two individuals that comes into play. The extended family—parents, siblings, and close friends—also partakes in the symphony of connections. Predictive analysis can help map out how the introduction of a new partner or a significant life event might influence these extended relationships, ensuring that the harmony of the group is maintained and that each member's role in the symphony is both recognized and cherished.

The Future of Love: A Tapestry Woven with Data

As we stand on the brink of a new era in relationship dynamics, predictive analysis offers a tapestry woven with the threads of data and human experience. It empowers us to look ahead, to anticipate the shifts in our emotional landscapes, and to approach the future of love with a blend of wisdom and wonder. While the heart may be a mystery that data alone cannot unravel, the insights gained from predictive models can lead us to a deeper understanding of the patterns that govern our affections, helping us to cultivate love that endures through the seasons of life.

Predictive analysis in the realm of love dynamics is not about reducing the richness of human emotion to mere numbers and charts. Instead, it's about enhancing our awareness of the potential paths our relationships might take. It's a tool that, when used with care and consideration, can help us foster stronger, more fulfilling connections with those we hold dear. As we continue to explore the frontiers of love and data, let us do so with the knowledge that each prediction is a stepping stone towards a more profound comprehension of the heart's timeless journey.

The Intricate Dance of Variables in Love's Equation

Love, much like the most complex of mathematical problems, is governed by a set of variables that can dramatically alter the outcome of any relationship. These variables act as the dynamic components of our emotional connections, constantly shifting and evolving in response to the myriad changes life throws our way. Understanding the role of these variables is crucial in maintaining a harmonious and fulfilling partnership.

The Fluid Nature of Love's Variables

In the grand scheme of love, variables are the unsung heroes that keep the balance. They are the subtle nuances that account for the ebb and flow of affection and commitment. **Time**, **attention**, and **emotional availability** are just a few examples of these pivotal elements that can be tweaked and transformed as circumstances dictate. Whether it's the arrival of a newborn, a sudden career opportunity, or the simple evolution of personal interests, these variables must be recalibrated to ensure that love doesn't just survive, but thrives.

Time: The Currency of Connection

Consider time as the currency through which we express our dedication to our partners. It's not just about the quantity of time spent together, but the quality of those moments. As life becomes busier, we might find ourselves needing to adjust how we allocate our time to ensure that our relationships do not suffer from neglect. It's about finding that sweet spot where both partners feel valued and important.

Attention: The Spotlight of Affection

Attention is another critical variable in the love equation. It's the spotlight we shine on our partners to show that we value their presence and contributions to our lives. When life's demands pull us in different directions, recalibrating our attention means being present during the moments we share, actively listening, and showing empathy. It's about making sure our partners feel seen and heard, even when our attention is divided.

Emotional Availability: The Heart's Open Door

Lastly, emotional availability is the open door to our hearts that invites our partners to seek refuge and support. It's about being there emotionally, not just physically. When faced with new challenges, such as a relocation or personal growth, our emotional availability may need to be adjusted to ensure that our partners don't feel isolated or disconnected from our inner world.

Adapting to Life's Symphony

The beauty of love's variables lies in their adaptability. They allow us to compose a symphony that resonates with the rhythms of our lives. By being mindful of these variables and willing to adjust them as needed, we can create a relationship that is both resilient and responsive to change. It's a delicate balancing act, but one that is essential for a lasting and loving partnership.

The role of variables in love equations is a testament to the fluidity and adaptability of love itself. They are the tools we use to fine-tune our relationships, ensuring that they can withstand the test of time and change. By understanding and adjusting these variables, we can navigate the complexities of love with grace and harmony, crafting a bond that is both strong and supple in the face of life's inevitable transformations.

The Constants of Love: Unchanging Pillars in the Dynamics of Affection

Love, in its myriad forms, is a complex and multifaceted emotion that has been the subject of countless poems, songs, and stories throughout human history. Yet, despite its complexity, there are elements within the concept of love that remain steadfast and unyielding. These constants form the bedrock of what could be termed the conservation theory of love, suggesting that no matter the trials and tribulations of life, the core capacity for love within each of us remains undiminished.

The Unchanging Nature of Love's Capacity

One of the most profound constants in the realm of love is the idea that our capacity to love does not wane with time or circumstance. This is the constant in the love equation, a fixed value that represents the potential each person has to give and receive love. It is a comforting thought that, regardless of the challenges we face or the losses we endure, our ability to love remains intact, ready to be tapped into and shared.

The Resilience of Love Through Life's Ups and Downs

Life is a rollercoaster of experiences, with its fair share of highs and lows. Yet, through this unpredictable journey, love's resilience shines as a beacon of hope. The constancy of love provides a sense of stability and assurance. It is the knowledge that, even when the world around us changes, the love we hold within and the love we share with others can endure. This enduring quality of love is a testament to its strength and its role as an anchor in our lives.

Love's Enduring Presence Across Time and Space

The constants of love transcend not only the fluctuations of our daily lives but also the boundaries of time and space. Love's presence is felt across generations, in the cherished memories of those who came before us and in the legacies we leave for those who follow. It is a thread that weaves through the tapestry of human existence, connecting us to each other in an unbreakable bond that defies the limitations of the physical world.

The Universal Language of Love

Love's constancy is also reflected in its universality. It is a language understood by all, regardless of culture, language, or background. This universal aspect of love allows us to connect with others on a fundamental level, fostering empathy, understanding, and compassion. It is a reminder that, at our core, we are all capable of experiencing and expressing this most human of emotions.

Nurturing the Constants of Love in Our Lives

While the constants of love are inherently present within us, they flourish most fully when nurtured. It is through our actions, our words, and our commitment to one another that these constants are brought to life. By recognizing and honoring the unchanging aspects of love, we can create strong, lasting relationships that withstand the test of time. It is our responsibility to cultivate these constants, to ensure that love's capacity continues to grow and enrich our lives and the lives of those around us.

The constants of love serve as the unwavering pillars upon which the complexities of human emotion are built. They remind us that, no matter what changes we face, the essence of love remains untouched. By embracing and nurturing these constants, we can ensure that love's presence in our lives is as enduring as the stars in the night sky, a perpetual source of light and warmth in an ever-changing universe.

Unveiling the Enigma: The Complexities of Measuring Love

Love, in its myriad forms, is the invisible thread that weaves through the tapestry of human experience, binding us in ways that are both profound and, often, ineffable. It is a universal language that transcends barriers, yet its quantification remains an elusive endeavor, fraught with challenges that intrigue both romantics and rationalists alike.

The Paradox of Quantifying the Unquantifiable

The quest to measure love is akin to capturing the essence of a sunset within a single equation; it is both a noble pursuit and a paradox. Love is not merely a static entity to be tallied but a dynamic interplay of emotions, actions, and connections that defy simple arithmetic. While researchers have attempted to model love using mathematical frameworks, these representations can only offer a shadow of love's true complexity.

The Limitations of Love Metrics

Consider the hypothetical scenario where a model predicts a waning of affection towards friends post-marriage. This might seem logical, as time and emotional investment are often redirected towards one's spouse. However, life is not a controlled experiment, and the model fails to account for the unpredictable nature of human relationships. A lifelong friend's unwavering support during a personal crisis can cause an unexpected surge in the emotional bond, a variable that no algorithm could have anticipated.

The Dance of Variables in Love's Equation

Love's equation is not one of constants but of ever-shifting variables. The intensity of love can fluctuate with a simple gesture, a word, or a shared memory. It is influenced by a constellation of factors, including personal history, individual needs, and the unique chemistry between people. These nuances are the brushstrokes of love's masterpiece, and they resist being distilled into cold, hard data.

The Spectrum of Love's Manifestations

Moreover, love is not a monolith but a spectrum that encompasses a range of emotions and connections. The love between friends, the passion between lovers, the devotion of a parent—all these are different hues of love, each with its own frequency and amplitude. To attempt to measure love is to try to apply a single scale to a rainbow of experiences, each as distinct as it is beautiful.

Embracing the Mystery Beyond the Numbers

Perhaps the true takeaway is that while we can endeavor to model love mathematically, we must acknowledge the element of mystery that love retains. It is this very unpredictability and depth that makes love so captivating. Love is not a commodity to be quantified but an experience to be cherished, a journey to be embarked upon with an open heart and a sense of wonder.

The Dance Continues: Love Beyond Measure

In the end, love's true measure is found not in the realm of numbers but in the immeasurable moments that define our lives. It is in the laughter shared with a friend, the comfort of a partner's embrace, and the silent understanding between kindred spirits. Love, in all its forms, remains a testament to the human spirit's capacity for depth, resilience, and transcendence. It is a dance to which we all know the steps, even if we can't quite count the beats.

The Delicate Dance of Heart and Mind: Navigating Love with Logic and Emotion

In the grand tapestry of human relationships, love often appears as a complex and enigmatic force, weaving together the threads of our most primal emotions with the intricate patterns of our rational thoughts. The interplay between heart and mind is not merely poetic musings but a tangible dynamic that can be approached with a blend of mathematical precision and emotional intelligence. This delicate balance is crucial in nurturing and sustaining meaningful connections.

Rationality Meets Romance: The Equation of Love

Imagine love as a formula, where every variable represents a component of our emotional and rational selves. It's a concept that might seem antithetical to the spontaneous nature of affection, yet it offers a unique perspective on managing the ebbs and flows of a relationship. Couples who embrace this mathematical approach to love are not reducing their feelings to cold calculations; rather, they are acknowledging that a successful partnership requires thoughtful consideration and emotional investment.

Love's Conservation: Balancing Time and Affection

Consider the principle of love's conservation, akin to the laws of physics that govern energy. In this context, it implies that the love within a relationship must be maintained through a careful distribution of time and attention. A couple might sit down to rationally discuss their weekly schedules, ensuring that both partners' needs are met. Yet, this logical planning is underpinned by a current of deep affection, a desire to prioritize their bond amidst life's relentless pace.

The Heart's Voice in a World of Logic

While the mind constructs a framework for the relationship, the heart infuses it with warmth and meaning. Emotions are the vibrant colors that fill the spaces between the lines of our logical blueprints. They remind us that at the core of every discussion, decision, and compromise, there is a fundamental drive to connect, to understand, and to love. It is the heart's voice that often guides us through the complexities of partnership, urging us to listen, empathize, and embrace.

The Synergy of Thought and Feeling

The true beauty of the interplay between heart and mind lies in their synergy. When a couple navigates their relationship with both an analytical and emotional lens, they create a robust foundation for growth. They learn to communicate effectively, addressing issues with a blend of practicality and sensitivity. This dual approach fosters a deeper understanding and respect for one another, allowing both partners to flourish individually and as a unit.

Practical Love: Tools for Harmony

Incorporating tools such as shared calendars, regular check-ins, and open dialogues can seem mundane, but they are the nuts and bolts that hold the structure of a relationship together. These practical elements provide clarity and prevent misunderstandings, creating a safe space for emotions to be expressed and appreciated. By valuing both the mind's insights and the heart's impulses, couples can navigate the unpredictable waters of love with a sense of direction and purpose.

Embracing the Complexity of Love

Ultimately, the interplay of heart and mind in love is a testament to the complexity of human relationships. It is a dance that requires patience, practice, and a willingness to learn from each step. By honoring both the logical and emotional aspects of our connections, we open ourselves to a more profound and fulfilling experience of love. So let us celebrate this intricate dance, for it is in the union of heart and mind that love finds its truest expression and its most enduring strength.

Reflections on the Universality of Love's Mathematics

Love, in its essence, is a universal language spoken by hearts across the globe. It is a force that knows no bounds, no cultural barriers, and certainly no personal prejudices. The mathematics of love, a concept both poetic and practical, suggests that there are underlying principles that govern the way we form and maintain relationships. These principles, much like the axioms of geometry or the laws of physics, apply to all, irrespective of where we come from or who we are.

The Equation of Emotional Balance

Consider the love equation as a tool for emotional balance. It's a formula that helps us measure and adjust the give-and-take in our relationships. This equation doesn't require us to be mathematicians; rather, it asks us to be mindful of the harmony between our emotional investments and returns. Whether you're from the bustling streets of New York or the serene landscapes of Kyoto, the love equation can guide you to healthier, more fulfilling connections.

Cultural Constants in Love's Calculus

The constants in love's calculus are the shared values and desires that bind us as humans. These include the need for companionship, understanding, respect, and affection. While the expressions of love may vary from culture to culture, the fundamental craving for connection is a common denominator. This universality allows us to apply the same mathematical principles to love, no matter the cultural context, and find common ground in the pursuit of lasting relationships.

Personal Variables and the Love Algorithm

While the constants remain fixed, the variables in the love algorithm represent our individual differences. Our personal experiences, preferences, and quirks all play a role in how we love and wish to be loved. The beauty of love's mathematics lies in its flexibility to accommodate these personal variables, enabling us to tailor our approach to love in a way that resonates with our unique selves and complements the uniqueness of others.

The Sum of Shared Experiences

The universality of love's mathematics is a testament to the shared human experience. It's a reminder that, at our core, we all speak the same emotional language. By embracing the mathematical principles of love, we can navigate the complexities of relationships with a sense of confidence and commonality. Love, much like the most elegant of equations, is a balance of constants and variables, a sum of shared experiences that unites us in our diversity.

Love's mathematics is not just a metaphor; it's a practical framework for understanding the dynamics of our most cherished connections. It's a universal language that, when spoken fluently, can lead to the most harmonious of human bonds.

As we journey through the pages, the narrative weaves together the precision of mathematics with the nuanced realm of our emotions. This compelling perspective offers a beacon of clarity in the often unpredictable seas of human relationships. By applying mathematical concepts to the ebbs and flows of love, we are afforded a lens through which we can predict, analyze, and even enhance our interactions with others. Embrace this opportunity to harness the power of numbers to navigate the complexities of love with confidence and foresight, enriching your life and the bonds you share with others.

Love derivatives

In the enchanting realm of emotions, if we dare to quantify the ineffable—love—much like a mathematician discerns the gradient of a curve, we stumble upon the concept of "Love Derivatives." Imagine charting the ebbs and flows of affection on a graph, where each point signifies the intensity of your feelings. The love derivative, then, becomes a poignant measure, capturing the very essence of how swiftly or gently your love for someone blossoms or fades with the passage of time.

This intriguing notion allows us to visualize love's dynamics in a new light. It's not just about the depth of love at any given moment, but the pace of its transformation that truly captivates the heart. Whether it's the exhilarating rush of new love that accelerates like a shooting star, or the steady, comforting decline of a love that has matured and settled into companionship, the love derivative maps the heart's silent whispers and its loudest beats, offering a unique glimpse into the temporal dance of our deepest human connection.

Understanding the Dynamics of Romance: The First-Order Love Derivative

When we delve into the realm of romance, the concept of the first-order love derivative emerges as a fascinating metaphor for the immediate rate of change in our feelings. Picture this: at the onset of a new relationship, there's an undeniable surge of excitement and passion. This intense burst of emotion can be likened to a high positive first-order derivative, signaling a steep and rapid climb in the intensity of love. It's that heart-racing, butterflies-in-the-stomach sensation that tells us we're experiencing something special and new.

As we navigate through the twists and turns of a relationship, the first-order love derivative serves as a mathematical mirror, reflecting the instantaneous fluctuations of our hearts. A high positive value might indicate those moments of joyous discovery and shared laughter, while a negative value could represent the cooling periods or the occasional disagreement. Understanding this concept doesn't just add a touch of whimsy to the way we view our relationships; it also offers a unique perspective on how love evolves over time, reminding us that change is the only constant in the equation of the heart.

Exploring the Dynamics of Affection: Navigating the Curves of Love's Acceleration

When we delve into the realm of relationships, we often speak of love as if it were a journey—a dynamic, evolving process that can ebb and flow with time. But what if we could quantify this journey, much like a physicist might measure velocity and acceleration? Enter the concept of second-order love derivatives, a fascinating metaphorical tool that helps us understand not just how love is growing, but the rate at which this growth is itself changing.

Imagine a blossoming romance where every shared moment and every whispered promise seems to draw two hearts closer at an ever-increasing pace. This is where the second-order derivative shines, offering a glimpse into the momentum of a couple's emotional connection. A positive second-order derivative in this context signifies that love is not only intensifying, but it's doing so with increasing vigor—each day brings a deeper, more profound level of commitment than the last. It's the difference between a steady walk hand-in-hand and a heart-racing sprint into each other's arms. As we navigate the complexities of human emotions, understanding the acceleration of love can be a powerful way to gauge the health and potential of our most cherished relationships.

Exploring the Intricacies of Emotion through Mathematics

When we delve into the realm of emotions, particularly love, we often find ourselves at a loss to describe its complexity. Yet, imagine if we could quantify the ebbs and flows of our affections, much like a mathematician discerns patterns within numbers. Higher-order derivatives, a concept borrowed from calculus, offer a fascinating lens through which to examine the intricate dance of love's dynamics. These mathematical tools allow us to model the subtle shifts and changes in our emotional landscape, providing a unique perspective on the patterns that govern our hearts.

Consider the journey of a long-term relationship, a tapestry woven with threads of joy, sorrow, passion, and comfort. The initial rush of love, akin to a steep curve on a graph, eventually gives way to a series of peaks and valleys—each representing the highs and lows that couples navigate over time. By applying the concept of higher-order derivatives, we can create a model that captures these nuanced variations, offering a deeper understanding of the forces at play. It's a testament to the power of mathematics to illuminate the most human of experiences, revealing the beauty and complexity that lie within the rhythms of love.

Key Insight: Navigating the Dynamics of Love with Calculated Awareness

Love, much like any complex emotion, is subject to change over time. By understanding the concept of love derivatives, we can gain a profound insight into the rate at which our feelings evolve within our relationships. This knowledge is not just theoretical; it has practical applications that can significantly enhance our emotional intelligence. For instance, if we detect a negative first-order derivative in our emotions—indicating a decrease in our feelings—it serves as an early warning system. This can encourage us to proactively engage with our partner to address underlying issues, fostering open communication and potentially preventing minor problems from turning into irreparable rifts.

Real-World Application: Proactive Relationship Management

Imagine you're charting the course of your relationship, and you notice a trend that suggests a cooling off of affection. This is where the practical implications of love derivatives come into play. By acknowledging this trend, you can initiate meaningful conversations, seek to understand your partner's perspective, and work together to rekindle the spark that brought you together. It's about using this analytical tool to create a responsive and nurturing environment for love to flourish. In essence, love derivatives empower us to become architects of our own emotional well-being, guiding us to build stronger, more resilient bonds with those we cherish.

Understanding Love Derivatives in Harmonizing Relationships

In the intricate dance of relationships, love derivatives act as a subtle yet powerful tool to maintain equilibrium. Imagine love as a dynamic force, one that ebbs and flows with the rhythms of life. Just as in calculus, where derivatives measure the rate of change, love derivatives gauge the shifting intensity of our affections across our personal connections. For instance, when you notice a gradual decline in the time and energy you're investing in your partner, mirrored by an uptick in the attention you're lavishing on your child, it's a clear indicator that recalibration is in order. This isn't about quantifying love but rather about being mindful of its distribution, ensuring that each cherished bond receives the nurture it deserves.

Striking the Right Balance with Love Derivatives

The key to using love derivatives effectively lies in observation and action. By staying attuned to the subtle shifts in our emotional investments, we can preempt feelings of neglect or resentment before they take root. It's about fostering an environment where love is not just present but is also distributed in a way that aligns with our evolving priorities and responsibilities. Remember, it's perfectly natural for the derivative of love to fluctuate; what's crucial is our willingness to adapt and redistribute our time, affection, and attention to reinforce the stability and happiness of all our relationships.

Understanding the Calculus of Emotions: A Quantitative Approach to Love

Have you ever considered measuring love as if it were a mathematical equation? The concept of *love derivatives* is a fascinating tool that allows us to do just that—quantify and meticulously examine the ebb and flow of romantic feelings. By applying this analytical approach, we can chart the progression of a relationship, much like a mathematician plots a curve on a graph. This innovative method provides a window into the underlying mechanics of our emotions, offering a glimpse into the current state and potential future of our romantic bonds.

Imagine being able to predict the ups and downs of your relationship with the precision of a seasoned trader analyzing the stock market! By mapping out the *love derivatives*, we can observe the rate of change in our feelings, helping us to understand the intensity and direction of our emotions over time. This insight can be incredibly valuable, acting as a diagnostic tool to assess the vitality of a relationship. Whether you're in the honeymoon phase or navigating through rough waters, understanding the calculus of emotions can empower you to make informed decisions about your love life, fostering a healthier and more fulfilling partnership.

Reflections on the Limits of Quantification

In our quest to understand the complexities of human emotion, we often turn to the precision of numbers. Yet, when it comes to the multifaceted nature of love, we find ourselves grappling with the reality that some things in life resist being distilled into mere figures. The concept of love derivatives is indeed an intriguing one, offering a fresh perspective on how we might attempt to chart the course of our most profound connections. However, it's important to recognize that the true essence of love, with all its depth and nuance, eludes complete quantification.

The beauty of love lies in its ability to be deeply felt rather than coldly calculated. The deepest bonds of love are those that are experienced in the richness of shared moments and the silent understanding between souls. These are the aspects of love that cannot be captured by numbers or graphs. They are the silent whispers of the heart that speak volumes more than any data set ever could. As we delve into the world of love derivatives, we must remember that they are but a shadow of love's true form, a mere echo of the symphony that plays within the human heart.

This exploration into the realm of quantifying love is not without merit. It provides a unique framework for examining the dynamic nature of love and its evolution over time. By applying mathematical concepts to our emotional experiences, we gain a new vantage point from which to view the intricacies of our relationships. Yet, it is crucial to approach this framework with the understanding that it is a complement to, not a replacement for, the rich tapestry of love's reality. In the end, the most profound elements of love will always remain beautifully indescribable, a testament to the boundless capacity of the human spirit to feel and connect.

Chapter 5: Love in Societal Context

We delve into the intricate tapestry of love as it weaves through the fabric of society. Love, an emotion often confined to personal relationships, extends its reach far beyond, influencing the very essence of community and national bonds. We examine the transformative power of love in fostering unity, understanding, and cooperation among diverse groups of people. By embracing the principles of compassion and empathy, societies can cultivate environments where love acts as a cornerstone for collective progress and harmony.

The exploration of love within a societal context reveals its potential to act as a catalyst for social change. When communities come together, driven by the common goal of mutual respect and care, they lay the groundwork for a more inclusive and supportive social structure. This chapter highlights inspiring examples of love in action, from small acts of kindness rippling through neighborhoods to grand gestures of goodwill between nations. The narrative underscores the importance of nurturing love not just in our homes but also in the public sphere, where its impact can be monumental.

Finally, we consider the challenges and rewards of integrating love into the broader societal narrative. In a world often divided by differences, love serves as a universal language that can bridge gaps and heal wounds. This chapter invites readers to reflect on the role love plays in their own lives and encourages them to extend that love outward, fostering a more compassionate and connected world. Join us on this journey as we uncover the profound influence of love on society and the endless possibilities it presents for a brighter, more united future.

Love Among Communities: Sharing and Caring

In the tapestry of human experience, the threads of love and compassion weave a pattern that holds communities together. When we speak of love within a community, we are not merely referring to romantic or familial affection, but to a broader, more inclusive kind of love. This love is characterized by sharing and caring, by the willingness to extend oneself for the well-being of others, and by the recognition that our lives are interconnected in profound ways.

The Essence of Community Love

Love in a community manifests in various forms, from the simple act of checking on a neighbor to the more complex systems of support during times of crisis. It is the heartbeat of communal life, pumping vitality and connection through the social body. A community that prioritizes love and compassion is one that understands the strength found in unity and the power of collective action. Such a community recognizes that every individual, regardless of their background or circumstances, is deserving of respect, support, and kindness.

Celebrating Togetherness

One of the most visible expressions of love among community members is the shared celebration of life's milestones and festivals. These joyous occasions are not just about the festivities themselves but about the spirit of inclusivity and togetherness they foster. Whether it's a neighborhood block party, a cultural parade, or a communal harvest feast, these events serve as reminders of our shared humanity and the joy that comes from caring for one another.

The Role of Service

Community service is another powerful demonstration of love in action. When individuals volunteer their time and resources, they are making a statement about the kind of community they wish to cultivate—one where generosity and altruism are the norm. This could take the form of organizing food drives, participating in clean-up efforts, or mentoring youth. Each act of service strengthens the bonds between community members and creates a ripple effect of goodwill and compassion.

Building a Supportive Network

At the core of a loving community is a robust support network that springs into action when members face hardship. This network is the safety net that catches those who might otherwise fall through the cracks. It's the group of neighbors who rally around a family that has lost their home to a fire, the community fund that helps cover medical expenses for those in need, or the local organizations that provide shelter and assistance to the homeless. These acts of caring are the glue that holds a community together during tough times.

The distribution of love within a community is a true measure of its heart and soul. It is a reflection of the values and priorities that its members hold dear. A community that actively engages in sharing and caring creates an environment where all can thrive. It is a place where the collective well-being is placed above individual gain, and where every act of kindness contributes to a larger story of hope and connection. Let us all strive to be part of such communities, for it is through love and compassion that we can build a better world for ourselves and future generations.

National and International Relations: The Macrocosm of Love

In the grand tapestry of global interactions, the intricate dance of national and international relations mirrors the delicate dynamics of love in our personal lives. Just as love requires a careful balance of give and take, so too do the diplomatic engagements between countries. The concept of love conservation suggests that the energy we invest in our relationships must be managed wisely to maintain harmony and mutual benefit. This principle is equally applicable to the geopolitical stage, where nations must navigate the complex web of alliances, trade agreements, and cultural exchanges.

The Diplomatic Balance of Attention

Consider the nuanced art of diplomacy, where countries, much like individuals in a relationship, must allocate their attention and resources thoughtfully. A nation might deepen its trade relations with one ally, potentially causing another to feel neglected. However, skilled diplomats understand that this is not a zero-sum game. Instead, they strive to distribute their efforts in a way that maintains overall stability and fosters a network of positive relationships. This balancing act is akin to ensuring that each person in a group of friends feels valued and heard, despite the natural ebb and flow of individual interactions.

The Ripple Effect of International Trade

Trade agreements serve as a prime example of love conservation on the international stage. When two countries enter into a trade partnership, they are essentially expressing a mutual commitment to support each other's economic well-being. This symbiotic relationship can lead to a flourishing of innovation, cultural exchange, and shared prosperity. However, it is crucial to manage these agreements with care, as the benefits must be distributed in a way that does not foster resentment or inequality. Just as in a loving relationship, where partners celebrate each other's successes, nations must find joy in the mutual gains achieved through cooperation.

Cultural Exchanges: The Heartbeat of Global Understanding

Cultural exchanges are the heartbeat of international relations, pulsing with the potential to build bridges of understanding and empathy. When nations share their art, music, literature, and traditions, they are extending an olive branch of friendship that transcends political boundaries. These exchanges cultivate a sense of global community, reminding us that despite our differences, we share a common humanity. In the same way that sharing personal stories can deepen love between individuals, cultural exchanges can strengthen the bonds between nations.

The Constant Effort of Diplomatic Love

The overall diplomatic effort, much like the constant nurturing required in a loving relationship, must remain steadfast. Nations must be proactive in their diplomatic endeavors, seeking out new opportunities for collaboration and addressing any issues that arise with compassion and understanding. This ongoing effort ensures that the fabric of international relations remains strong and resilient, capable of withstanding the inevitable challenges that arise. Just as love in our personal lives requires patience, forgiveness, and a willingness to grow together, so too does the love shared between nations.

The principles of love conservation offer a profound lens through which we can view the relationships between nations. By applying the same care, balance, and commitment that we cherish in our personal connections, we can foster a world where international relations are characterized by mutual respect, shared prosperity, and enduring peace. Let us embrace the macrocosm of love in all our interactions, both personal and global, for it is through this universal language that we can truly unite and thrive.

The Impact of Social Policies on Love Allocation

In the intricate tapestry of society, the threads of love and care are woven through the fabric of our daily interactions. It's a profound truth that government policies, often seen as distant and impersonal, have the power to shape the contours of these emotional exchanges. The way love is allocated within a community can be subtly, yet significantly, influenced by the legislative frameworks that govern us.

Government's Role in Nurturing Compassion

Take a moment to consider the essence of love: it is the warmth of a community that supports its members, the hand that feeds the hungry, and the shelter that protects the vulnerable. Social welfare programs, designed to uplift the underprivileged, are a manifestation of this communal love. By ensuring that everyone has access to basic needs, these policies are not just redistributing resources; they are redistributing care, attention, and, ultimately, love.

A Minimum Level of Care for All

Imagine a society where no one falls through the cracks, where every individual is guaranteed a minimum level of dignity and care. This is the vision that drives many social policies. By providing assistance to those in need, whether through healthcare, education, or financial support, governments can create a safety net that catches those who might otherwise be neglected. This is love in action, a tangible expression of the value we place on each member of our society.

Bridging the Gap

It's important to recognize that love is not just a private affair but a public commodity that can be nurtured or neglected by policy decisions. When social programs bridge the gap between the haves and the have-nots, they foster a sense of belonging and community. This is crucial because when people feel cared for by their society, they are more likely to contribute positively to it, creating a virtuous cycle of love and support.

The Ripple Effect of Compassionate Policies

The impact of these policies extends beyond the immediate recipients of aid. When a child receives a quality education, when a family is lifted out of poverty, when the sick are healed, the benefits ripple outwards. Each act of support is a seed of love that can grow and spread, touching lives and shaping futures. In this way, the careful crafting of social policies is not just a matter of economics or politics; it is the art of cultivating love across a society.

The influence of social policies on love allocation is profound and far-reaching. By understanding and harnessing this power, governments have the opportunity to not only meet the material needs of their citizens but to also nourish the very bonds that hold us together. It is through these acts of collective care that we can build a society where love is not a scarce resource but a shared abundance.

The Ripple Effect of Societal Love: A Catalyst for Community Transformation

Introduction to the Power of Collective Compassion

In the intricate web of society, each thread of kindness weaves a pattern of profound impact, creating a tapestry of communal harmony that resonates through the lives of its members. The concept of societal love – the collective expression of empathy, care, and support – is not merely an idealistic notion but a practical catalyst for positive change. When we engage in acts of love and kindness, we initiate a ripple effect that can significantly enhance the overall quality of life within our communities.

The Transformative Impact of Public Spaces

Consider, for example, the transformative power of urban planning that prioritizes communal well-being. A city's initiative to create more public spaces like parks and community centers is not just an investment in infrastructure; it's an investment in the heart of the community. These spaces become arenas for connection, where residents of all ages and backgrounds can come together to share experiences, support one another, and foster a sense of belonging. The laughter of children playing, the quiet conversations between neighbors, and the shared celebrations of community achievements are the harmonious melodies that compose the symphony of societal love.

Strengthening Community Bonds Through Shared Experiences

The beauty of these shared spaces lies in their ability to break down barriers and build bridges. When people from diverse walks of life interact in a positive environment, they learn from each other and grow together. This mutual understanding and respect are the cornerstones of a strong community. As residents become more invested in their community's well-being, they are more likely to participate in local initiatives, volunteer their time, and contribute to the common good. This collective effort not only improves the physical aspects of the community but also fortifies the emotional and social support systems that are essential for a thriving society.

The Enduring Legacy of Kindness

The ripple effect of societal love extends beyond the immediate benefits. Each act of kindness plants a seed of compassion that can flourish for generations. Children who grow up witnessing and participating in acts of love and kindness are more likely to carry those values into adulthood, perpetuating a cycle of caring and community-mindedness. The enduring legacy of societal love is a community that values each member, recognizes the importance of collective well-being, and actively works towards a brighter future for all.

Embracing the Ripple Effect for a Better Tomorrow

The ripple effect of societal love is a powerful force that can transform communities from the inside out. By embracing acts of love and kindness, we can create a nurturing environment where every individual feels valued and connected. The creation of public spaces is just one example of how we can foster these connections and strengthen the bonds within our society. As we continue to spread love and kindness, we contribute to a more compassionate, resilient, and vibrant community, setting the stage for a better tomorrow for everyone.

Remember, the journey towards a loving society begins with a single act of kindness. Let us all be the pebble that creates ripples of change, echoing through the hearts and lives of those around us.

Exploring the Intricacies of Measuring Societal Love

Measuring love within a society is a task that is as intricate as it is essential. Love, in its purest form, is an emotion that transcends mere numbers and data points. It is a force that binds communities, heals wounds, and fosters growth. Yet, in our quest to understand the collective health of our societies, we attempt to quantify this unquantifiable sentiment.

The Challenge of Quantifying Compassion

The challenge lies in the subjective nature of love. What constitutes an act of love for one may not resonate the same way with another. Traditional metrics such as volunteer hours and charitable donations are often used as proxies to gauge a society's love. These indicators, while useful, fall short of capturing the full spectrum of compassion that thrives within a community. They are but a glimpse into the vast landscape of human kindness.

Beyond Numbers: The Depth of Societal Love

To truly measure love on a societal level, we must look beyond the numbers. We must consider the silent acts of kindness that occur daily, the support systems that go unnoticed, and the strength of relationships that bind people together. These elements of love are felt rather than tallied, experienced rather than calculated. They are the threads that weave the fabric of a loving society.

The Role of Subjective Measures

In recognizing the limitations of objective data, we must also embrace subjective measures. Surveys and interviews that capture personal experiences and perceptions of love can offer valuable insights. These narratives can help us understand the nuances of societal love and the impact it has on individuals and communities alike. They remind us that the essence of love is found in the stories we share and the lives we touch.

Embracing the Complexity of Love

While it is challenging to measure love on a societal scale, it is a pursuit that holds great significance. By acknowledging the complexity of this task and seeking a balance between objective and subjective approaches, we can gain a more holistic view of the love that underpins our societies. It is through this understanding that we can foster a world where love is not just measured, but truly cherished and cultivated.

The Collective Heartbeat: A Symphony of Compassion

Understanding Our Shared Pulse

The essence of a community's spirit is often likened to a *collective heartbeat*, a rhythm that resonates with the shared experiences and emotions of its members. This metaphorical pulse is a testament to the underlying unity that binds individuals together, reflecting the aggregate of our capacities for empathy, compassion, and love. When we consider the collective actions of a society, we are essentially observing this heartbeat in motion, a dynamic expression of our communal life force.

The Power of Unity in Action

Consider, for instance, the heartwarming solidarity displayed by a nation in the wake of a natural disaster. It's in these moments of crisis that the collective heartbeat is most palpable. Neighbors, strangers, and friends unite, channeling their individual strengths and resources into a powerful force for recovery and support. This spontaneous surge of collective action is a profound demonstration of our shared humanity, showcasing how, together, we can overcome adversity and foster hope amidst despair.

Small Acts, Big Impact

It's not just in times of crisis that the collective heartbeat is felt. Every day, small acts of kindness contribute to this rhythm, creating a melody of goodwill that echoes throughout society. Whether it's a smile offered to a stranger, a helping hand extended to someone in need, or a word of encouragement to a friend, these gestures may seem insignificant on their own. Yet, when multiplied by millions, they create an overwhelming force for good, a testament to the power of our collective spirit.

Cultivating Compassion

To nurture this collective heartbeat, it is essential that we each take responsibility for our part in the symphony. By cultivating our individual capacities for love and empathy, we contribute to the strength and resilience of our society. It is through education, open dialogue, and a commitment to understanding one another that we can enhance this collective pulse, ensuring that it beats strongly and steadily, guiding us towards a more harmonious and compassionate world.

The Echo of Our Actions

The collective heartbeat is more than just a metaphor; it is the very essence of our social fabric. It is the echo of our actions, the rhythm of our intentions, and the melody of our interactions. As we move forward, let us be mindful of the power we hold within us to influence this heartbeat. Let us strive to make it a rhythm of kindness, a beat of generosity, and a pulse of love that can be felt by all. For in the end, the health of our collective heart is the true measure of our society's vitality and the legacy we leave for future generations.

Reflections on Global Love Dynamics

In a world that's more connected than ever, the concept of love has evolved to encompass a broader, more inclusive spectrum. The dynamics of love are no longer confined by geographical borders or cultural barriers. Instead, they are influenced by global events and trends that shape our collective consciousness. As we witness movements for human rights and environmental protection gaining momentum, it's clear that love has the power to transcend national boundaries and unite people in common causes.

The Power of Collective Compassion

The surge of global movements is a testament to the power of collective compassion. When people from different corners of the world come together to fight for human rights or to protect our planet, it's a profound expression of love. This love is not romantic or familial; it's a love for humanity and the Earth that sustains us. It's a love that recognizes no borders, a love that speaks a universal language of empathy and solidarity.

Uniting for a Common Cause

The beauty of this global love dynamic is that it brings together individuals from diverse backgrounds. Whether it's advocating for social justice or rallying against climate change, these causes create a sense of unity and shared purpose. This unity is a powerful force, capable of sparking significant change and inspiring hope in a world that often seems divided.

Love Beyond Borders

As we reflect on the impact of global love dynamics, it's important to acknowledge that love can indeed be a catalyst for change. The emotional bonds that form between people fighting for a better world are a reminder that, at our core, we all share common values and aspirations. Love, in its most expansive form, has the potential to bridge the gap between nations and cultures, creating a more compassionate and connected global community.

Embracing a Global Perspective

The dynamics of love on an international scale are a powerful reminder of our interconnectedness. By embracing a global perspective on love, we open ourselves to new possibilities for collaboration and understanding. Let us continue to nurture this global love, for it is through this profound connection that we can hope to build a brighter, more harmonious future for all.

Chapter 6: The Global Love Equilibrium

We delve into the fascinating interplay between the Theory of Conservation of Love and its profound implications for international relations and the nuanced art of global diplomacy. At its core, this theory suggests that love, much like energy, is not lost but rather transformed and redistributed within the geopolitical landscape. We'll examine historical case studies and contemporary scenarios to illustrate how this concept shapes the bonds between nations.

Through a tapestry of diplomatic anecdotes and expert analysis, we uncover the subtle yet powerful ways in which the Theory of Conservation of Love manifests in the strategies and outcomes of international negotiations. Whether it's through the mutual respect between state leaders or the shared humanitarian efforts that transcend borders, this theory offers a unique lens through which we can understand the ebb and flow of global harmony and conflict.

Finally, we'll reflect on the potential of this theory to inspire a new paradigm in diplomatic engagement. By embracing the principles of empathy, reciprocity, and emotional intelligence, policymakers and diplomats alike can forge more meaningful and lasting alliances. Join us as we explore the transformative potential of love in the realm of international relations, where every act of kindness and cooperation can ripple outwards to create a more peaceful world.

International Diplomacy and Love Conservation

In the intricate dance of international relations, the concept of love conservation offers a unique perspective on how countries manage their diplomatic affections. Much like the careful conservation of natural resources, nations must judiciously allocate their goodwill, or 'love,' to foster alliances, soothe tensions, and maintain a harmonious global balance. This delicate act of balancing relationships is akin to an art form, where strategic displays of favor are both a necessity and a skill.

Strategic Alliances and Balancing Acts

Consider the scenario where a country finds itself in the midst of rising hostilities with a neighboring state. In response, it might bolster its ties with a friendly nation, thereby creating a counterweight to the brewing conflict. This strategic move is not unlike a chess player thinking several moves ahead, anticipating the opponent's strategy and adjusting accordingly. By strengthening one alliance, the nation effectively distributes its diplomatic 'love' to maintain equilibrium, ensuring that its overall international standing remains stable and secure.

The Ripple Effect of Diplomatic Decisions

The impact of such diplomatic decisions can ripple through the international community, influencing trade, security, and even cultural exchanges. When a country extends an olive branch to another, it is not merely a gesture of goodwill but a calculated investment in future cooperation. This investment can yield dividends in the form of mutual support in global forums, shared intelligence, and preferential trade agreements. The conservation of 'love' in diplomacy is, therefore, not only about maintaining balance but also about building a foundation for prosperity and peace.

The Human Element in International Relations

At the heart of international diplomacy lies the human element, where relationships between nations are ultimately shaped by the people who represent them. The conservation of 'love' in this context is a reminder that, despite the high stakes and complex strategies, diplomacy is driven by human emotions and the universal desire for understanding and respect. By approaching diplomatic relations with empathy and a genuine willingness to find common ground, nations can transcend political differences and cultivate a more compassionate and interconnected world.

The art of love conservation in international diplomacy is a testament to the nuanced and dynamic nature of global relations. It underscores the importance of strategic thinking, the interconnectedness of nations, and the human desire for harmony. As countries navigate the ever-shifting landscape of international politics, the careful allocation of their diplomatic 'love' will continue to be a defining factor in their success and the collective well-being of the world.

Case Study: Shifting Alliances and Love Rebalances

In the intricate dance of international relations, the concept of 'love' between nations often manifests as strategic alliances and partnerships. These relationships are not static; they evolve with the changing tides of political, ideological, and economic landscapes. This case study delves into the dynamic nature of these alliances and how they reflect the rebalancing of interests and priorities among nations.

The Cold War: A Chessboard of Shifting Loyalties

During the Cold War, the world witnessed a dramatic series of shifts in alliances. Nations were drawn into the orbit of either the United States or the Soviet Union, aligning themselves along ideological lines that often dictated their foreign policies and international relationships. However, these alliances were not set in stone. Countries recalibrated their stances based on a myriad of factors, including economic benefits, security guarantees, and political leverage. This period serves as a prime example of how the global balance of 'love'—or more aptly, strategic interest—can pivot in response to the geopolitical climate.

The Dance of Diplomacy in Modern Times

In today's world, the dance of diplomacy continues with new players and renewed considerations. Economic interdependence, regional conflicts, and the rise of non-state actors have all contributed to a complex web of relationships that can change with surprising speed. Nations now consider a broader range of factors, such as climate change agreements, cyber security threats, and the need for sustainable development, when forming or dissolving alliances. This contemporary landscape illustrates that the rebalancing of 'love' between nations is an ongoing process, influenced by both enduring interests and emerging global challenges.

Lessons Learned and Future Implications

The historical and contemporary shifts in alliances teach us that the concept of 'love' between nations is a metaphor for the pragmatic and often transactional nature of international relations. As global dynamics continue to evolve, it is crucial for policymakers to remain agile and responsive to the changing currents of diplomacy. Understanding the lessons of the past can help in navigating the complexities of the future, ensuring that alliances are formed with both strategic wisdom and a forward-looking vision.

The shifting alliances and the rebalancing of 'love' between nations underscore the fluidity of international relations. As we examine historical patterns and contemporary trends, it becomes clear that alliances are not merely about affection or sentimentality; they are about the calculated pursuit of national interests. By studying these shifts, we gain valuable insights into the forces that drive nations together or apart, and we learn to anticipate the potential realignments that shape our world.

Future Trends: Globalization and Its Effect on Love Distribution

In an ever-shrinking world, where distances are reduced to mere clicks and the exchange of ideas is as swift as the speed of light, globalization has emerged as a force majeure, reshaping not just economies and politics, but the very fabric of human relationships. The concept of 'love'—once confined by geographical and cultural boundaries—is now experiencing a renaissance of its own, as it becomes a currency exchanged across the globe with newfound fluidity.

The Global Heartbeat: Love Without Borders

As the tendrils of globalization reach further into the corners of our lives, they weave a complex tapestry of connections that transcend traditional notions of love. The digital age has ushered in an era where love letters are replaced by instant messages, and romantic serenades are shared as playlists across streaming platforms. This new paradigm has democratized love, making it more accessible, yet also more challenging to navigate. The internationalization of love means that people are forming bonds that are not just romantic, but also platonic and professional, with individuals from vastly different backgrounds.

The Cultural Exchange: Love's New Lexicon

The exchange of culture that comes hand-in-hand with globalization has enriched the language of love, infusing it with diverse expressions and practices. Valentine's Day, for instance, once a Western tradition, is now celebrated across continents, while matrimonial customs from one culture find echoes in another. This cross-pollination of love's expressions has broadened our understanding and appreciation of the emotion, allowing for a more inclusive and expansive view. However, it also poses the challenge of preserving the uniqueness of local love traditions in the face of a homogenizing global culture.

The Balancing Act: Navigating the Global Love Market

With the world's heartstrings intertwined more closely than ever, the distribution of love has become a delicate balancing act. Relationships now must consider not only personal and cultural differences but also the global implications of their love. The rise of international dating apps and websites is a testament to the global market for love, where the search for a soulmate knows no borders. Yet, this also raises questions about the sustainability of long-distance relationships and the emotional toll of navigating time zones and cultural gaps.

The Future of Love: Embracing Globalization's Embrace

Looking ahead, the effect of globalization on love distribution is poised to evolve in ways we can only begin to imagine. As we become more interconnected, the potential for international and intercultural relationships will likely increase, offering opportunities for love that is enriched by diversity. The challenge will be to foster these relationships in a way that respects individual and cultural differences while celebrating the common human experience of love. In this global village, love is not just a private affair but a global phenomenon that can bridge divides and bring people together in a world that needs unity more than ever.

Globalization has indeed complexified the distribution of love, creating a world where the heart knows no frontiers. As we navigate this brave new world, it is essential to remember that love, in its essence, remains a universal language that can unite us across all divides. Embracing the changes and challenges that come with globalization can lead to a richer, more diverse understanding of love, one that holds the promise of a more connected and compassionate global community.

The Role of International Organizations: Fostering Global Harmony

International organizations are the architects of peace and cooperation in the modern world. They serve as the backbone for fostering global harmony, ensuring that the spirit of unity transcends borders. These entities are not just bureaucratic bodies; they are the collective voice of humanity, striving to create a world where every nation can share in the bounty of peace and prosperity.

Uniting Nations in the Pursuit of Peace

One of the most prominent examples of such an organization is the United Nations (UN). The UN stands as a beacon of hope, a place where countries come together to weave a tapestry of solidarity. It's a unique platform where nations can voice their concerns, celebrate their diversity, and find common ground. Through its various humanitarian and peacekeeping missions, the UN embodies the essence of international cooperation, distributing the 'love' that binds us all. This love manifests in the support provided to those in need, whether it's through disaster relief, advocating for human rights, or fostering sustainable development.

Bridging Divides Through Diplomacy and Aid

International organizations also play a pivotal role in bridging the divides that often separate nations. By facilitating dialogue and understanding, they help to prevent conflicts and mediate resolutions. Organizations like the International Red Cross and Red Crescent Movement, for instance, provide a neutral ground for humanitarian aid, regardless of political affiliations or borders. Their work in conflict zones and in the aftermath of natural disasters is a testament to the power of compassion and the universal language of humanitarianism.

Championing Sustainable Development for All

Sustainable development is another critical area where international organizations shine. The World Bank and the International Monetary Fund (IMF), for example, work tirelessly to promote economic stability and growth. They provide financial resources and expertise to countries in need, helping to lift populations out of poverty and onto a path of sustainable prosperity. By focusing on long-term development goals, these organizations contribute to a more equitable world, where every individual has the opportunity to thrive.

A Symphony of Cooperation

The role of international organizations cannot be overstated. They are the conductors of a global symphony, orchestrating efforts to ensure that the melody of peace and love resonates in every corner of the planet. Through their dedication to diplomacy, humanitarian aid, and sustainable development, these organizations help to maintain the delicate balance of international relations. They remind us that, despite our differences, we are all part of the same human family, and it is only by working together that we can create a harmonious future for generations to come. Let us continue to support and celebrate the invaluable work of these organizations, for they are the pillars upon which our global love equilibrium rests.

Economic 'Love': The Delicate Dance of Trade and Investment

In the intricate ballet of international relations, economic ties are often likened to a form of 'love' – a symbiotic connection that, when well-nurtured, can lead to mutual prosperity and understanding. This economic 'love' is not merely about the exchange of goods and services; it's about building relationships that transcend borders, fostering trust, and investing in a shared future. However, like any relationship, it requires a delicate balance, one that harmonizes with a nation's broader interests and strategic goals.

The Balancing Act of National Interests and Economic Bonds

Imagine a country as a suitor, courting partners with whom it can exchange not just commodities, but also ideas, culture, and innovation. This courtship, however, is not without its complexities. A nation must often weigh its economic desires against other critical factors such as security, diplomacy, and environmental sustainability. For instance, while a country might be tempted to engage in lucrative trade deals with a resource-rich nation, it must also consider the long-term implications of such a partnership on its energy independence and ecological commitments.

Strategic Trade to Offset Economic Challenges

Consider the scenario where a country faces an economic slump due to trade disputes with a key partner. In this delicate situation, the nation in question might seek to diversify its economic 'love' by increasing trade with another nation, thereby cushioning the blow of the downturn. This strategic move is akin to keeping the flames of economic passion alive by exploring new relationships, ensuring that the country's overall economic health remains robust. It's a dance of diplomacy and economics, where each step is carefully calculated to maintain balance and forward momentum.

Investment: The Long-Term Commitment in Economic 'Love'

Trade might be the initial spark in the economic 'love' story, but investment is the long-term commitment that cements the relationship. When a country decides to invest abroad, it's making a profound statement of trust and confidence in the future of that economic partnership. These investments can take many forms, from infrastructure projects to joint ventures in technology and research. They create jobs, spur innovation, and weave the economies of nations together in a tapestry of shared success. But as with any commitment, these investments must be made judiciously, with an eye toward how they align with the nation's values and the well-being of its citizens.

The economic 'love' that nations share through trade and investment is a powerful force, one that can lead to a more interconnected and prosperous world. Yet, it must be pursued with care, always in concert with other national interests. As countries navigate this complex relationship, they must remain attuned to the nuances of diplomacy, the imperatives of security, and the demands of global stewardship. Only then can the full potential of economic 'love' be realized, bringing with it the promise of a brighter, more collaborative future.

Environmental 'Love': A Tapestry of Shared Responsibility

In the heart of every individual lies the capacity for profound care and stewardship for our planet. This intrinsic 'love' for the environment is not just a personal sentiment but a shared responsibility that binds us all. It is a collective duty that transcends borders, cultures, and societies, urging us to act in harmony for the greater good of our world. The environmental challenges we face today are not isolated issues; they are interconnected threads in the delicate tapestry of Earth's ecosystem. To preserve and nurture this tapestry, we must weave together our efforts, ensuring that every strand of action contributes to a sustainable future.

The Paris Agreement: A Symbol of Collective Commitment

The Paris Agreement on climate change stands as a testament to what can be achieved when nations unite in a common cause. This landmark accord is a pledge by the global community to share the 'love' for our planet through concrete actions. By aiming to limit global warming and reduce greenhouse gas emissions, the agreement acknowledges that the health of our environment is a shared concern that requires a shared solution. Each country's commitment to adjust its own carbon footprint is a step towards a collective healing of the Earth. It is a powerful example of how shared responsibility can manifest in global policies and inspire individual actions.

The Ripple Effect of Individual Actions

While international agreements are crucial, the true power of environmental 'love' is often found in the everyday choices of individuals. Each decision to recycle, to conserve water, to choose sustainable products, or to advocate for green policies is a ripple that spreads across the pond of collective consciousness. These ripples can merge to form waves of change, influencing communities, industries, and governments. By embracing our personal responsibility to the environment, we contribute to a larger movement—a movement that is capable of transforming the way we interact with our planet. It is through these small, consistent acts of care that we can make a significant impact on the health of our environment.

Cultivating a Culture of Environmental Stewardship

To truly embed environmental 'love' into the fabric of society, we must cultivate a culture that values and prioritizes the Earth's well-being. Education plays a pivotal role in this cultural shift, as it equips individuals with the knowledge and tools to make informed decisions. Schools, communities, and media outlets have the power to raise awareness and foster a sense of responsibility towards the environment. By highlighting the interconnectedness of all living things, we can encourage a mindset that sees environmental care not as a burden, but as a natural extension of our existence. It is through this cultural transformation that we can nurture a generation of environmental stewards, ready to protect and cherish our planet.

The 'love' we share for our environment is a force that can unite us in action and purpose. It is a shared responsibility that calls for collaboration, commitment, and continuous effort. From the global stage of the Paris Agreement to the individual choices we make each day, every action counts. By weaving together our collective and individual efforts, we can create a sustainable future for our planet—a future where the tapestry of Earth's ecosystem remains vibrant and whole for generations to come. Let us embrace this responsibility with open hearts and determined spirits, for the love of our environment is the love of life itself.

Consider the dynamics between nations: just as individuals seek affirmation and reciprocity in their relationships, so do countries. A nation's sense of 'love'—manifested through diplomatic recognition, fair trade, and cultural respect—needs to be acknowledged. When a nation perceives this 'love' as being unreturned, it can lead to a sense of injustice and imbalance. This perceived deficit may ignite defensive postures or even aggressive actions in an attempt to restore equilibrium or assert dominance.

The conservation of love theory thus provides a unique lens through which we can analyze international relations. It encourages us to look beyond the surface of military might or economic power and consider the emotional and psychological undercurrents that influence state behavior. By recognizing the importance of emotional reciprocity on a global scale, we can begin to identify the root causes of conflicts and, more importantly, find pathways to sustainable peace.

In essence, the pursuit of peace is not merely a political or strategic endeavor but a deeply human one that requires empathy, patience, and a willingness to understand the 'other.' As we reflect on the causes of peace and conflict, let us remember that at the core of every society lies the universal need for love and recognition. By fostering these values within and between nations, we may move closer to a world where conflict is the exception, not the norm, and where peace is cultivated with the same care and intention as the most cherished relationships in our lives.

Chapter 7: Navigating the Complexities of Love's Conservation

We delve into the heart of the debate surrounding the Theory of Conservation of Love. We'll explore the spectrum of critiques that challenge the theory's foundations, offering a comprehensive and nuanced perspective on its strengths and weaknesses. By examining the theory through the lens of its critics, we aim to shed light on the complex dynamics that govern the conservation of love in human relationships.

While the Theory of Conservation of Love has been a beacon for understanding emotional continuity, it's not without its detractors. We'll dissect the most compelling arguments against the theory, considering the diverse contexts in which love's conservation may falter or thrive. This critical analysis is not just an academic exercise; it's a journey towards a deeper understanding of love's role in our lives.

Finally, we'll discuss the limitations of the theory in practical applications. Recognizing that no single theory can encapsulate the vastness of human emotions, we'll consider alternative viewpoints and theories that complement or contrast with the conservation perspective. Our goal is to leave you with a richer, more layered appreciation of the challenges and opportunities in preserving love's essence in a constantly changing world.

Anomalies and Exceptions: When Love Seems Infinite

Love, in its purest form, is often described as an unquantifiable force, transcending the ordinary limits we encounter in life. It's a phenomenon that defies the usual constraints, suggesting that in certain exceptional cases, love can indeed seem infinite. This concept challenges our understanding of emotional resources, pushing us to reconsider the boundaries of affection and care.

The Boundless Nature of Parental Love

Consider the profound and unwavering love a parent feels for their child. This type of love is frequently cited as a prime example of love's boundless potential. It's a love that doesn't keep score, doesn't wane with time, and doesn't falter under pressure. It's as if the very essence of a parent's love for their offspring is to be inexhaustible, a testament to the idea that love, in some instances, can be limitless.

Love as a Renewable Resource

The notion that love is a finite resource is often rooted in our experiences of scarcity and loss. Yet, the way love manifests in certain relationships suggests that it operates more like a renewable resource, replenished by acts of kindness, empathy, and understanding. When we witness the lengths to which individuals will go for those they love, it becomes clear that love's capacity to grow and regenerate is one of its most miraculous qualities.

Embracing the Infinite

Embracing the concept of infinite love requires a shift in perspective. It invites us to view love not as a commodity to be conserved, but as an ever-flowing wellspring that can nourish and sustain us through life's challenges. It's a perspective that encourages generosity of spirit and an open heart, reminding us that when we give love freely, we are not left with less, but are often rewarded with more.

In the dance of life, love's anomalies and exceptions are the moments that take our breath away. They are the instances that inspire us, that remind us of the profound depth of the human heart. When we encounter love in its most boundless form, we are witnessing the extraordinary capacity for human connection—a force that, against all odds, appears truly infinite.

Understanding the Complexity of Love: A Discourse on Criticisms and Counterarguments

Love, as a profound human emotion, has been the subject of countless discussions, debates, and analyses. Critics often highlight that love, unlike a physical entity, defies quantification and the laws of conservation. They argue that love's intangible nature places it beyond the realm of empirical measurement and scientific scrutiny. This perspective raises intriguing questions about the essence of love and its impact on human relationships.

The Spontaneity of Love: A Challenge to Quantification

One of the most compelling arguments against the quantification of love comes from the phenomenon of love at first sight. This sudden and intense emotional connection challenges the notion that love is a resource that can be depleted or divided among different relationships. Critics suggest that the spontaneous emergence of love in such scenarios indicates that love is not a finite commodity but rather an unlimited, dynamic force that can manifest unexpectedly and without apparent cause.

The Multidimensional Nature of Love

Proponents of love's immeasurability often emphasize its multidimensional nature. Love encompasses a spectrum of feelings, actions, and commitments that vary greatly from person to person and relationship to relationship. This diversity makes it difficult to create a universal metric for love. Instead, love is better understood as a unique and personal experience that resists standardization and remains largely subjective.

The Interplay of Love and Relationships

While some argue that love cannot be conserved, others observe that love's expression often changes as it is shared among different relationships. For example, the love one feels for a romantic partner may differ in intensity and expression from the love felt for a friend or family member. This adaptability suggests that while love itself may not be quantifiable, its manifestations can be observed and appreciated in the context of interpersonal dynamics.

The debate over the quantification of love opens up a fascinating dialogue about the nature of human emotions and relationships. While critics maintain that love cannot be measured like a physical quantity, the spontaneous and multidimensional aspects of love provide a rich tapestry of experiences that continue to inspire and challenge our understanding of this most enigmatic of emotions.

Revisiting the Theory: Adaptations and Extensions

In the ever-evolving landscape of human psychology, theories that once seemed concrete are now being challenged and refined. The understanding of human emotions, in particular, has revealed a complexity that demands our theories adapt and extend to encompass these new insights. As we delve deeper into the intricacies of the human heart, we find that our previous models may require significant adjustments to remain relevant and accurate.

The Dynamic Nature of Love

One of the most profound emotions we experience is love. Traditional theories often paint love as a static emotion with a fixed capacity. However, recent observations suggest that love is far more dynamic. It is not a finite resource but rather a growing, evolving force that can deepen and expand over time. This realization calls for a reevaluation of our theoretical frameworks to account for love's fluid distribution and its potential for growth through new experiences and relationships.

Emotional Complexity and Theoretical Adaptability

The takeaway from this ongoing discourse is clear: our theories must be adaptable. They should be flexible enough to incorporate the nuances of human emotions like love. For instance, the idea that love can grow over time is a significant departure from the notion of a static emotional capacity. This suggests that as individuals encounter new experiences, their ability to love can increase, reshaping the distribution of their emotional investments and attachments. Such an extension to existing theories not only makes them more robust but also more reflective of the human experience.

Expanding the Capacity for Love

To illustrate this point, consider the example of a person who, after a significant life event such as traveling or overcoming a challenge, finds their capacity for love to be greater than before. This person may discover new depths of empathy and connection that were previously untapped. By adjusting our theories to consider these possibilities, we acknowledge that love is not a static emotion but one that can be cultivated and nurtured over time, much like a garden that flourishes with care and attention.

Embracing a Holistic Approach

The journey of revisiting and refining our theories is an ongoing process that mirrors the complexity of human emotions. As we strive to understand the full spectrum of human experience, it is essential that our theoretical models evolve alongside our growing knowledge. By embracing a holistic approach that recognizes the adaptability and expansion of emotions like love, we can develop a more nuanced and comprehensive understanding of the human heart. This, in turn, will enable us to foster deeper connections and enrich our collective experience of life's most profound emotion.

The Role of Altruism and Philanthropy: A Heartfelt Journey Beyond Self

In the tapestry of human experience, the threads of altruism and philanthropy weave a pattern of profound generosity and compassion. These acts of selflessness are the embodiment of a love that transcends the boundaries of personal relationships, reaching out to touch the lives of strangers with the same warmth and care that we extend to our nearest and dearest.

The Essence of Altruism: Love Without Borders

Altruism, at its core, is the selfless concern for the well-being of others. It is a noble trait that drives individuals to act for the benefit of someone else, without any expectation of reward or recognition. This pure form of giving is not just a moral choice but a testament to the human capacity for unconditional love.

Takeaway: When we engage in altruistic behaviour, we demonstrate that our capacity for love is not a finite resource. Rather, it is an ever-expanding force that grows stronger with each act of kindness.

Philanthropy: The Power of Purposeful Giving

Philanthropy takes altruism to a structured level, where individuals or organizations make concerted efforts to bring about positive change. Philanthropists channel their resources—be it time, money, or expertise—towards causes that resonate with their values, often addressing social issues on a grand scale.

Example: Consider the philanthropist who donates to build schools in underprivileged areas. This act not only reflects a commitment to education but also a belief in the potential of every child to thrive when given the opportunity.

The Ripple Effect: How Giving Benefits All

The beauty of altruism and philanthropy lies not only in the immediate impact they have on recipients but also in the ripple effect they create. Each act of generosity inspires others, fostering a culture of giving that can transform communities.

Takeaway: The benefits of altruism and philanthropy extend beyond the material. They enrich the giver's life, bringing a sense of fulfillment and connection to a larger purpose.

Balancing Personal Love with Universal Love

One might wonder if giving to others takes away from the love we have for our family and friends. The answer is a resounding no. The human heart has an incredible capacity to love on multiple levels simultaneously.

Example:A parent who volunteers at a local shelter is not loving their child any less. In fact, they are setting an example of empathy and responsibility that can strengthen the bond within the family.

Embracing a Life of Giving

The role of altruism and philanthropy in our lives is not just about the acts themselves but about the message they convey. They remind us that we are all connected and that by helping others, we are also helping ourselves. As we navigate through life's journey, let us carry the torch of generosity, lighting the way for a kinder, more compassionate world.

Takeaway: Whether through small acts of kindness or grand gestures of support, every contribution counts. By embracing the spirit of altruism and philanthropy, we can all play a part in creating a legacy of love that endures.

Love's Multiplicative Effect: The Ripple of Compassion

Understanding the Abundance of Love

Have you ever considered the idea that love, unlike material resources, doesn't diminish when shared but instead grows and expands? It's a heartwarming realization that when we give love, we're not slicing up a pie that will eventually run out. Instead, we're kindling a flame that can grow into a roaring fire, warming not just one, but many. This is the essence of love's multiplicative effect.

The Power of One Act of Kindness

Imagine you decide to spend a few hours each week volunteering at a local shelter. Initially, it might seem like a small drop in the ocean of need. However, this single act of kindness is far from insignificant. As you give your time and compassion to those in need, something remarkable happens within you. Your heart expands, your understanding deepens, and your capacity to care extends beyond the walls of the shelter.

A Chain Reaction in Personal Relationships

This newfound depth of compassion doesn't stay confined to the volunteer work. It follows you home, to work, and into your social circles. The patience and understanding you've cultivated begin to influence your interactions with friends, family, and even strangers. Your relationships are enriched as you approach them with the same empathy you've shown to those at the shelter. Love, in its most beautiful form, begins to multiply, touching lives in ever-widening circles.

The Misconception of Love's Scarcity

Many of us operate under the misconception that our emotional resources are limited, that if we give too much to one person or cause, we'll have less available for others. But love defies this logic. It operates on a principle of abundance, not scarcity. The more love you give away, the more you find you have to offer. It's a renewable resource that feeds on its own generosity.

Embracing the Infinite Potential of Love

So, let's challenge ourselves to reject the scarcity mindset and embrace the infinite potential of love. By doing so, we unlock a powerful force for good in our lives and the lives of others. Whether it's through volunteering, lending a listening ear, or simply offering a smile, every act of love sets off a chain reaction of positivity. Remember, when it comes to love, the whole is always greater than the sum of its parts.

Love's multiplicative effect is a testament to the boundless nature of the human heart. When we give love freely, we don't just fill others' cups—we create an overflowing fountain of compassion that can rejuvenate a parched world. Let's make the conscious choice to be conduits of this incredible force, and watch as the ripples of our actions spread far and wide.

The Influence of Cultural Narratives on Our Understanding of Love

Unveiling the Power of Cultural Narratives

Cultural narratives are the tapestries upon which societies paint their values, beliefs, and expectations. These stories, passed down through generations, are not merely entertainment; they are the lenses through which we view the world, including the multifaceted emotion of love. The way we perceive and experience love is deeply intertwined with the cultural narratives that we absorb from a young age. These narratives can either limit or expand our understanding of love's potential, influencing whether we see it as a finite resource or an infinite blessing.

Love's Abundance vs. Scarcity: A Cultural Perspective

Consider the profound impact of cultural narratives on our perceptions of love's availability. In some cultures, love is akin to an inexhaustible well, ever-flowing and enriched by each act of sharing. This perspective fosters a sense of abundance, encouraging individuals to express love freely without fear of depletion. On the other hand, other cultures may adopt a more conservative stance, treating love as a precious commodity that must be guarded and rationed. This scarcity mindset can lead to a guarded heart, where love is doled out sparingly, often with the worry that it might run out.

Contrasting Cultural Views on Love

To illustrate, let's delve into an example. In many Eastern cultures, the concept of love is often intertwined with duty, family honor, and collective well-being. Love is not just an individual emotion but a communal bond that strengthens as it is shared among family members and the community. This collective approach to love emphasizes its growth through mutual support and shared experiences. Conversely, Western narratives sometimes promote a more individualistic view of love, highlighting the pursuit of romantic love as a personal journey and achievement. This can sometimes lead to the notion that love is a zero-sum game, where one's gain is another's loss, inadvertently fostering a sense of scarcity.

Redefining Love Through Cultural Exchange

The beauty of our interconnected world lies in the opportunity to redefine these narratives through cultural exchange. As we encounter diverse perspectives on love, we can challenge our preconceived notions and perhaps adopt a more holistic view. By embracing the idea that love can be both a personal journey and a communal experience, we can transcend cultural limitations and enrich our understanding of love. This synthesis of ideas can lead to a more nuanced appreciation of love's abundance, where it is not only found in romantic partnerships but also in the warmth of friendship, the solidarity of community, and the selflessness of compassion.

Embracing Love's Infinite Possibilities

Cultural narratives play a pivotal role in shaping our perceptions of love. By recognizing and reflecting on these influences, we can consciously choose to embrace a narrative of abundance. Love, in its truest form, is not a finite resource to be hoarded but a boundless force that grows with every act of kindness and connection. Let us celebrate the diversity of love's expressions and allow ourselves to be vessels through which love's infinite possibilities can flow.

Takeaway: By understanding and embracing the diverse cultural narratives about love, we can enrich our lives with a more abundant and inclusive perspective, fostering connections that transcend cultural boundaries and nourish the soul.

Reflections on the Universality of Love

Love, an emotion as old as humanity itself, is often considered a universal experience. However, the expression and understanding of love can vary dramatically across different cultures and individuals. This diversity challenges the notion that love is a monolithic concept, experienced and expressed uniformly across the globe.

The Cultural Lens of Love

In collectivist societies, where the group's needs often take precedence over the individual's, love is frequently seen as a duty and a commitment to the family and community. This contrasts with individualist societies, where love is often associated with personal fulfillment and emotional satisfaction. The cultural lens through which we view love shapes not only how we express it but also how we expect to receive it.

Love's Many Forms

Love manifests in a myriad of forms, from the passionate bonds between romantic partners to the deep affection between friends and the unconditional love of a parent for a child. Each form of love carries its own set of expectations and norms, which can be further influenced by cultural practices and societal values. Recognizing this multiplicity is essential in understanding the complex tapestry of human emotions.

The Language of Love

Language plays a pivotal role in how we communicate and understand love. Words and phrases that describe love in one language may not have direct equivalents in another, leading to a rich diversity in the expression of love. This linguistic variation reminds us that love is not only felt but also articulated in countless ways, shaped by the tongues we speak.

Love's Evolution

As societies evolve, so do their conceptions of love. Globalization and the blending of cultures bring about new interpretations and expressions of love. While the essence of love may remain constant, its manifestations are ever-changing, reflecting the dynamic nature of human societies.

Embracing Love's Diversity

The universality of love is not found in a single, unchanging experience but in the shared capacity to feel and express this profound emotion. By embracing the diversity of love's expressions, we gain a deeper appreciation for the myriad ways in which it enriches our lives. Love, in its essence, is a mosaic made up of different shapes and colors, each piece contributing to the beauty of the whole.

Chapter 8: Enriching Lives with the Theory of Conservation of Love

We delve into the heartwarming applications of the Theory of Conservation of Love, exploring its transformative power in our daily interactions, educational environments, and healing spaces. Discover how this profound theory can elevate your life and the lives of those around you.

Everyday Enchantment: Love in Daily Life

Imagine starting each day with a renewed sense of purpose and connection. We'll guide you through simple yet impactful ways to integrate the Theory of Conservation of Love into your routine, creating ripples of positivity that can profoundly affect your personal and professional relationships.

Educational Empowerment: Shaping Hearts and Minds

Educators play a pivotal role in nurturing young hearts. This section provides innovative strategies for incorporating the principles of love conservation into curricula and classroom management, fostering an atmosphere where empathy and understanding flourish alongside academic achievement.

Therapeutic Transformation: Healing with Heart

Therapists and counselors will find valuable insights on how to weave the Theory of Conservation of Love into their practice, offering clients a pathway to healing that is grounded in compassion and emotional resilience. Learn techniques that can help unlock the healing potential of love in therapeutic settings.

Implementing Love Conservation in Daily Life

Love, much like any precious resource, requires careful management and conservation to flourish. By integrating the principles of love conservation into our daily routines, we can foster deeper connections and ensure that our relationships remain vibrant and fulfilling. Here's how you can start to practice love conservation and make every interaction count.

Mindful Relationship Management

Takeaway: Embracing the concept of love conservation can transform the way we approach our relationships, leading to a more balanced and intentional way of connecting with those around us.

Example: Consider setting aside dedicated time each week to spend with loved ones, free from the distractions of work or technology. This could be as simple as a family game night or a coffee date with a friend. The key is to be fully present during these moments, allowing you to cultivate a deeper bond and appreciation for one another.

Quality Time Allocation

Takeaway: Allocating quality time is not just about quantity; it's about the value and intention behind the time spent with each significant person in our lives.

Example: You might create a small ritual that holds special meaning, such as a nightly walk with your partner or a weekly phone call to a distant family member. These consistent acts of love demonstrate your commitment and help maintain a strong emotional connection, even when life gets busy.

Balancing Acts

Takeaway: Love conservation is about finding equilibrium. It's recognizing that while our time and emotional energy are finite, our capacity for love is not.

Example: Strive to balance your attention among all your relationships. This might mean learning to say no to certain social obligations to prioritize family time or ensuring that your friendships are nurtured alongside your romantic relationship. Remember, it's the quality of the interactions, not just the frequency, that counts.

Incorporating love conservation into your daily life is a journey of mindfulness and intention. It's about recognizing the value of each relationship and making conscious choices to nurture them. By doing so, we not only enrich our own lives but also create a ripple effect of positivity and connection that can extend far beyond our immediate circle. Start today, and watch as your relationships bloom with renewed energy and affection.

Understanding the Heart of Education: Balancing Emotional Investments through Learning

In the intricate tapestry of modern education, there lies an opportunity to weave in the golden threads of emotional intelligence and empathy. Educational systems are not just about imparting knowledge; they are about shaping individuals who can navigate the complexities of human relationships with grace and understanding. By integrating the principles of love conservation into the curriculum, we can teach our students the art of maintaining a healthy emotional equilibrium in their lives.

Social-Emotional Learning: The Key to Harmonious Relationships

Imagine a classroom that goes beyond the traditional subjects and delves into the realm of social-emotional learning (SEL). This innovative approach equips students with the tools to understand and manage their emotions, set and achieve positive goals, feel and show empathy for others, establish and maintain positive relationships, and make responsible decisions. By incorporating SEL into the school curriculum, we foster an environment where students learn to balance their emotional investments, ensuring that their connections with friends and family are nurtured and sustained.

The Ripple Effect of Empathy in Education

When students learn about the conservation of love, they begin to see the world through a lens of compassion and empathy. This perspective is not confined to the classroom; it extends to every interaction they have, creating a ripple effect that can transform communities. By teaching our young ones the importance of emotional balance, we are setting the stage for a future where interpersonal relationships are valued and preserved. This is the kind of education that doesn't just produce scholars but also cultivates wise, caring citizens.

A Call to Action for Educational Systems

It is time for educational systems to embrace the concept of love equilibrium as a fundamental aspect of learning. By doing so, we are not just educating minds; we are nurturing hearts. This holistic approach to education can create a more empathetic and socially skilled generation, ready to lead with love and understanding. Let us commit to this vision and watch as our students grow into well-rounded individuals who are as adept at managing their emotions as they are at solving complex equations.

Therapy and Counseling: Restoring Balance in Love

Navigating the complexities of relationships can often feel like walking a tightrope. It's a delicate balance of give and take, understanding, and compromise. Therapy and counseling offer a supportive environment where individuals and couples can learn to restore equilibrium in their love lives. By engaging with a therapist, clients can explore the underlying issues that may be causing disharmony and work towards a more balanced and fulfilling relationship.

The Role of Therapists in Fostering Relationship Balance

Therapists are like architects of emotional well-being, helping clients to construct a more stable foundation for their relationships. They employ various theories and techniques to assist individuals in understanding their emotional needs and the dynamics at play within their partnerships. By identifying patterns of behavior that contribute to imbalance, such as codependency or unequal emotional investment, therapists can guide clients towards healthier interactions and a more equitable distribution of emotional energy.

Practical Applications in Therapy Sessions

In a typical session, a therapist might encourage clients to reflect on how they allocate their emotional resources. For example, if a client is pouring all their emotional energy into their partner while neglecting their own needs, the therapist can help them recognize this pattern. Together, they can work on strategies to ensure that the client's emotional well-being is not sidelined. This might involve setting boundaries, developing self-care routines, or learning to communicate more effectively with their partner about their needs.

Takeaways for a Harmonious Relationship

The ultimate goal of therapy in the context of relationships is to empower clients to create a more balanced and harmonious connection with their partner. By addressing issues such as codependency, therapists can help clients to redistribute their emotional energy in a way that is both healthy for themselves and nurturing for the relationship. As clients learn to balance their own needs with those of their partner, they pave the way for a more stable and loving bond. Remember, a balanced relationship is not about keeping score; it's about creating an environment where both partners feel valued, heard, and connected.

The Essential Interplay Between Self-Care and Nurturing Love

In the intricate dance of life, where we often juggle multiple roles and responsibilities, the concept of self-care can sometimes be relegated to the background. However, it is crucial to understand that self-care is not a luxury but a fundamental aspect of sustaining our ability to share love and compassion with others. When we prioritize our well-being, we are not being selfish; rather, we are ensuring that we have the emotional, physical, and mental resources to give the best of ourselves to those we cherish.

Recharging Emotional Batteries Through Self-Care

Imagine your capacity to love as a wellspring of energy. Just like any source of power, it can deplete if not replenished. Self-care serves as the charger for your emotional batteries. By dedicating time to activities that nurture your soul, you allow yourself to regain strength and vitality. Whether it's a quiet walk in the park, a relaxing bath, or indulging in a hobby, these moments of self-care are not acts of indulgence but necessary pauses that enable you to be more attentive, patient, and affectionate in your interactions with loved ones.

The Ripple Effect of a Well-Cared-For Self

When you are well-cared-for, the benefits extend beyond your personal sphere. It creates a ripple effect that touches the lives of those around you. A person who is content and at peace with themselves radiates positivity and is better equipped to handle the stresses that come with relationships. This doesn't mean that challenges won't arise, but a well-nourished spirit is more resilient and can approach conflicts with a clearer mind and a more loving heart. Your self-care practices, therefore, are not just for you—they are a gift to those you love, allowing you to distribute love more generously and thoughtfully.

Cultivating a Sustainable Love Through Self-Care

Ultimately, the practice of self-care is about cultivating a sustainable form of love. It's about recognizing that you cannot pour from an empty cup and that taking care of yourself is the first step in being able to take care of others. By integrating self-care into your daily routine, you ensure that your capacity to love remains abundant and that your relationships are nurtured by a wellspring of compassion and vitality. Remember, the love you give to yourself is the love you are able to share with the world, making self-care an indispensable part of love distribution.

Work-Life Balance and Love Conservation: The Art of Harmonizing Professional and Personal Fulfillment

In the bustling rhythm of modern life, the quest for a harmonious work-life balance has become more crucial than ever. It's a delicate dance between professional responsibilities and personal relationships, where the concept of love conservation plays a pivotal role. Love conservation isn't just about romantic love; it's about nurturing and preserving the affection and care we have for those who matter most in our lives. By consciously allocating our time and energy, we can ensure that our work does not overshadow the precious moments we share with our loved ones.

Crafting the Perfect Schedule: A Working Parent's Guide

Imagine a working parent, juggling the demands of a career while striving to be present for every milestone in their child's life. It's a scenario that many can relate to, and it requires a strategic approach to time management. By creating a well-thought-out schedule that includes dedicated family time, parents can safeguard the reservoir of love for their children. This might mean setting aside certain evenings for family dinners, attending weekend sports games, or establishing a nightly bedtime story ritual. These moments, consistently reserved for family, become the building blocks of a strong and enduring bond.

The Ripple Effect of Balanced Priorities

When we achieve a balance between our work and personal lives, the benefits extend beyond our immediate circle. Colleagues and employers often notice the positive impact of a well-rounded individual who brings a sense of calm and focus to the workplace. Similarly, children who observe their parents managing time effectively learn valuable lessons about setting priorities and respecting boundaries. This ripple effect can lead to healthier work environments and more resilient family dynamics, as everyone involved understands the importance of nurturing relationships alongside professional growth.

Embracing Flexibility for Sustainable Love Conservation

It's important to recognize that the equilibrium of work-life balance is not a one-size-fits-all solution. Life is unpredictable, and there will be times when our carefully laid plans need to adapt to unforeseen circumstances. Flexibility is key in these moments, allowing us to recalibrate and continue practicing love conservation without guilt or stress. By being adaptable, we demonstrate to our loved ones that while work is important, it will never take precedence over the love and attention they deserve. In this way, we can maintain a sustainable balance that honors our commitments both at work and at home, ensuring that neither sphere is neglected.

The art of balancing work and life is indeed a form of love conservation. It's about making intentional choices that prioritize our relationships, while still achieving professional success. By mastering this balance, we not only enrich our own lives but also set a powerful example for those around us.

Embracing Community Engagement: A Journey of Love and Connection

Community engagement is not just about volunteering or participating in local events; it's a profound journey that allows us to channel our love and compassion into the world around us. By stepping out of our personal bubbles, we can transform our understanding of love from a private emotion to a public expression that enriches our lives and the lives of others.

The Heart of Community: Expanding Our Circle of Love

When we think of love, we often picture the intimate bonds we share with family and friends. However, the essence of love is not confined to those closest to us. By engaging with our community, we can broaden the scope of our affection. **Community service projects**, such as organizing a local clean-up or volunteering at a food bank, allow us to extend our love to the wider community. This act of giving not only benefits those we help but also nurtures a sense of belonging and shared purpose within ourselves.

The Ripple Effect: How Small Acts of Love Can Transform a Community

Every act of kindness, no matter how small, has the potential to create a ripple effect throughout the community. When we contribute our time and energy to community initiatives, we're not just helping others; we're also setting an example and inspiring those around us to join in the effort. This creates a powerful cycle of love and support that can revitalize neighborhoods, foster mutual respect, and bridge divides. It's a testament to the idea that love, when shared freely, grows exponentially.

The Takeaway: Love as a Collective Experience

Community engagement is a beautiful and effective way to allocate our love beyond our immediate circles. It's about recognizing that our capacity for love is limitless and that when we invest it in our communities, we can achieve remarkable things. Whether it's through mentoring youth, supporting local businesses, or simply being a friendly face to a neighbor, every action contributes to a more loving and connected world. Let's embrace this opportunity to spread love far and wide, for the betterment of all.

The Art of Love Maintenance

Love, in its myriad forms, is the invisible thread that weaves through the tapestry of our lives, binding us together in a complex yet beautiful pattern. To keep this thread strong and vibrant requires more than just passive existence; it demands an active, ongoing commitment to nurturing and understanding. This is the art of love maintenance, a skill that, when mastered, can lead to a lifetime of fulfilling relationships and unbreakable bonds.

Conscious Effort: The Heartbeat of Relationships

Every relationship, be it romantic, familial, or platonic, thrives on the lifeblood of conscious effort. It's not enough to simply feel love; we must also act on it. This means taking the time to truly listen to our loved ones, to communicate openly and honestly, and to show appreciation for their presence in our lives. It's the small, daily acts of kindness and consideration that accumulate over time, building a foundation of trust and affection that can weather any storm.

Reflection: The Mirror of Growth

Reflection is the mirror that allows us to see the growth in our relationships. It involves looking inward to understand our actions, motivations, and feelings, as well as outward to recognize the needs and desires of those we love. By regularly assessing the state of our relationships, we can identify areas that require attention or change. This reflective practice is not about finding fault or assigning blame, but about fostering an environment where love can flourish and evolve.

Balance: The Dance of Harmony

Love is a delicate dance that requires balance. It's about giving and receiving in equal measure, about knowing when to lead and when to follow. In the hustle and bustle of daily life, it's easy to lose sight of this equilibrium. We must be vigilant in ensuring that our relationships are not one-sided, that the scales of love are not tipped too far in any one direction. This balance is not static; it's a dynamic, ever-shifting state that demands our attention and adjustment.

The Art in Practice: A Lifelong Journey

The art of love maintenance is not a destination but a journey, one that lasts a lifetime. It's about embracing the imperfections and celebrating the triumphs, about learning from the lows and savoring the highs. Each relationship is a unique masterpiece, a work of art that we co-create with those we hold dear. By committing to the practices of conscious effort, reflection, and balance, we can ensure that the art of love maintenance is not just an ideal to aspire to, but a reality we live every day.

Reflections on Love's Impact on Well-being

Love, an emotion as old as humanity itself, weaves through our lives, shaping our experiences and coloring our perceptions. It is a force so potent that its presence, or absence, can profoundly affect our mental, emotional, and even physical states. The warmth of love's embrace has the power to elevate our well-being, creating ripples of positivity that extend beyond the individual to the community at large.

The Ripple Effect of Love

Consider the way love acts as a balm for the soul, soothing our inner turmoil and providing a sanctuary of comfort and acceptance. **Studies have consistently demonstrated** that individuals who are enveloped in love, whether it be through familial bonds, romantic connections, or deep friendships, often report heightened levels of happiness and a robust sense of satisfaction with life. This isn't mere coincidence; it's the manifestation of love's transformative power.

Love as a Pillar of Health

But love's influence isn't confined to our emotional landscape; it also plays a pivotal role in our physical health. The security that comes from loving relationships can lower stress levels, reduce the risk of heart disease, and even bolster our immune systems. It's as if love wraps us in a protective cocoon, shielding us from the harsh elements of life's uncertainties. In this way, love is not just a feeling but a foundation upon which we can build a healthier, more resilient self.

Cultivating a Community of Care

On a communal level, love's impact is equally profound. When love is freely given and received within a community, it fosters an environment where individuals feel valued and supported. This sense of belonging can lead to increased cooperation, stronger social bonds, and a collective resilience that benefits everyone. It's a testament to the idea that love, when shared, has the capacity to uplift not just individuals but entire communities, creating a harmonious and nurturing space for all.

In essence, love is more than just a private emotion reserved for the few; it is a universal currency of well-being that enriches our lives in countless ways. By recognizing and embracing the power of love, we can enhance our own well-being and contribute to a more loving, supportive world. Let us not underestimate the value of love; instead, let us distribute it generously, knowing that with each act of love, we are weaving a tapestry of well-being that can cover the world.

Teaching Love Conservation to Children: Strategies for Balanced Relationships

In the journey of nurturing well-rounded individuals, imparting the wisdom of love conservation to children is paramount. This concept revolves around the understanding that our reservoirs of time and emotional energy are finite, necessitating judicious allocation to maintain harmony in our various relationships. Below are sophisticated strategies to guide children in mastering the art of love conservation.

1. The Power of Storytelling

Narratives are a profound medium for conveying life lessons. **Craft tales** that depict protagonists who adeptly navigate their affections and attentions among family, friends, and acquaintances. For instance, a narrative centered on a youngster who learns to equitably distribute their time between a new sibling and longstanding friendships can offer valuable insights. Such stories not only entertain but also serve as a blueprint for children to emulate.

2. Role-Playing as a Learning Tool

Role-playing exercises are an interactive approach to understanding the consequences of our choices on interpersonal dynamics. By simulating scenarios where children must prioritize their time among loved ones, they gain firsthand experience in managing their relationships. This method fosters empathy and decision-making skills, allowing children to appreciate the delicate balance required in nurturing connections.

3. Engaging in Meaningful Discussions

Open dialogues about emotions and relationships are crucial. Pose reflective inquiries such as, "How do you surmise your friend feels when you dedicate time to them?" or "In what ways can we demonstrate our affection to various family members?" These conversations encourage children to contemplate the emotional ramifications of their actions and to develop a considerate approach to distributing their love.

4. Observational Learning Through Modeling Behavior

Children are astute observers, often emulating the behaviors of adults around them. **Demonstrate how you manage your own relationships**—the division of time between your partner, friends, family, and self-care—and articulate the significance of such balance. This not only provides a practical example for children to follow but also reinforces the concept through visible action.

5. Cultivating Emotional Intelligence

Activities designed to enhance emotional intelligence are instrumental in teaching children about empathy and the importance of considering others' feelings. Through games and exercises that promote understanding and perspective-taking, children can better grasp the nuances of love conservation. This foundation is essential for them to appreciate the impact of their attention and affection on others.

6. Practical Skills for Love Conservation

"Time management" is a tangible skill that aids in love conservation. Utilize tools such as calendars or planners to visually demonstrate how children can segment their time among school, family, friends, and personal interests. Additionally, emphasize that love is not solely quantified by time spent together but also by the quality of interactions. Teach them diverse expressions of love, from acts of kindness to words of affirmation.

By weaving these methodologies into daily learning experiences, children can cultivate a sophisticated understanding of relationships and the art of maintaining a healthy equilibrium of love and attention. It is imperative to customize these discussions to align with the child's age and developmental stage, ensuring the concepts are conveyed in an accessible and relatable manner. Through these efforts, we can guide the next generation in building fulfilling and balanced relationships.

Chapter 9: Teenage Love and the Rebalancing of Affections

We delve into the intricate tapestry of teenage love, examining its volatile nature and its place within the broader context of the Theory of Conservation of Love. This theory posits that love, akin to energy, is neither created nor destroyed but rather redistributed across relationships and life stages. Teenage love, with its intense emotions and formative experiences, serves as a critical juncture in this ongoing process of emotional reallocation.

The episode begins by dissecting the psychological underpinnings of teenage love, characterized by a maelstrom of hormones and the quest for identity. Adolescents, caught in the throes of self-discovery, often project their inner turmoil onto their romantic entanglements, thus amplifying the intensity of their affections. We scrutinize the ways in which these burgeoning emotions align with the Theory of Conservation of Love, suggesting that the fervor of teenage romance is a necessary precursor to the maturation of one's capacity to love.

Furthermore, we explore the social implications of teenage relationships, acknowledging the role of peer influence and cultural expectations in shaping young individuals' perceptions of love. The chapter provides a critical analysis of how these external factors can distort the natural rebalancing of affections, potentially leading to a misallocation of emotional resources that may echo into adulthood. It is within this framework that the conservation of love is tested, as teenagers navigate the complex interplay between personal feelings and societal norms.

Finally, the episode concludes with a discussion on the transformative power of teenage love. Despite its potential for tumult, it is an essential phase in the emotional development of individuals. Through the lens of the Theory of Conservation of Love, we posit that the experiences garnered during this period lay the groundwork for more stable and enduring relationships in the future. As such, teenage love is not merely a fleeting fancy but a fundamental component in the lifelong journey of emotional equilibrium.

The Intricacies of Adolescent Affection

Adolescence heralds a transformative era in emotional maturation, wherein the phenomenon of teenage love emerges as a pivotal aspect of this developmental journey. This period is characterized by a burgeoning capacity for deep emotional connections, often culminating in the formation of romantic relationships that signify a profound shift in the allocation of affection. Such relationships, while a natural progression in the emotional evolution of a young person, can have far-reaching implications on their social dynamics and interpersonal priorities.

The Reconfiguration of Emotional Investments

The advent of romantic interests during teenage years frequently leads to a reallocation of time and emotional energy. A teenager may find themselves increasingly drawn to their partner, investing considerable effort in nurturing this newfound connection. This shift often manifests in a reduction of time previously dedicated to familial interactions, as the adolescent navigates the delicate balance between the comfort of family bonds and the excitement of romantic exploration. The redistribution of love, therefore, is not merely a transfer of time but a complex renegotiation of emotional priorities.

The Impact on Familial Relationships

The reorientation of a teenager's love can sometimes be misconstrued as a withdrawal from family life. However, it is essential to recognize this phase as a natural extension of the individual's growth. As adolescents forge their identities and explore intimate relationships, the time and attention once reserved for family may diminish, but this does not necessarily equate to a diminution of familial love. Rather, it is an expansion of the adolescent's emotional repertoire, accommodating new forms of affection while learning to maintain established familial ties.

Navigating the Emotional Tapestry of Teenage Love

Teenage love is an integral component of the emotional tapestry that constitutes human development. As adolescents embark on this journey, they encounter the complexities of balancing newfound romantic interests with existing familial bonds. It is a delicate dance of emotional reallocation that, when navigated with care and understanding, can enrich the teenager's capacity for love and empathy. Thus, the emergence of teenage love is not merely a redistribution but an expansion of the heart's capacity to embrace the multifaceted nature of human affection.

Parental love serves as the cornerstone of emotional development for adolescents, shaping their perceptions and behaviors in future romantic engagements. The depth and nature of affection and support provided by parents can significantly mold a teenager's expectations and interaction patterns within their own relationships. A nurturing and secure home environment typically fosters self-esteem and teaches constructive communication and conflict resolution skills, which are vital for healthy romantic connections.

Conversely, a lack of parental warmth and responsiveness can leave teens feeling emotionally deprived, prompting them to seek solace and acceptance in their peer groups or romantic partners. This quest for validation can lead to a heightened vulnerability to peer pressure and a propensity to enter into relationships prematurely, without the necessary emotional maturity or self-awareness. Such teens may also struggle with setting appropriate boundaries, which is crucial for any balanced and respectful relationship.

Moreover, the parental model of love and relationships sets a precedent for what teenagers consider normal and acceptable. Adolescents who witness positive relationship dynamics, characterized by mutual respect, trust, and affection, are more likely to emulate these traits in their own romantic endeavors. In contrast, exposure to dysfunctional parental relationships can predispose teens to replicate similar patterns of behavior, potentially perpetuating a cycle of unhealthy relationships.

The influence of parental love on a teenager's approach to romantic relationships is profound. It is incumbent upon parents to provide a foundation of love and guidance that not only nurtures their child's growth but also equips them with the emotional intelligence to navigate the complexities of romantic relationships. As such, fostering a supportive and open family environment is paramount in preparing adolescents for the challenges and joys of building meaningful connections with others.

Understanding the Impact of Peer Influence on Adolescent Romantic Relationships

Adolescence is a critical period for social development, where individuals are particularly susceptible to the influences of their peer groups. This is especially true in the context of romantic relationships. Teenagers often look to their peers for guidance and validation, which can significantly shape their attitudes and behaviors towards love and partnership. The dynamics within a peer group can either positively or negatively affect a teenager's perception of what constitutes a healthy relationship.

For instance, a teenager might feel compelled to enter into a relationship due to overt or subtle pressure from friends, or the pervasive desire to conform to the group's norms. This external influence can lead to a misalignment between a teenager's personal readiness for a relationship and the expectations set by their peers. Consequently, the authenticity and balance of love in their life may be compromised, as the relationship is not solely based on genuine feelings, but rather on the need to fit in or gain social approval.

Moreover, peer groups can serve as an echo chamber for ideas and behaviors related to love and relationships. If a peer group holds certain beliefs about dating, such as the importance of being in a relationship to maintain social status, teenagers may adopt these beliefs without critical examination. This can result in a superficial understanding of love, where the depth and complexity of emotions are overshadowed by the pursuit of social acceptance.

The influence of peers on teenage love is a multifaceted issue that warrants careful consideration. Educators, parents, and mentors should strive to foster environments where adolescents feel empowered to make decisions about relationships based on their own values and readiness, rather than the pressures imposed by their peer group. By encouraging self-reflection and open communication, we can help teenagers navigate the intricate world of love with greater confidence and self-awareness.

The Pivotal Role of Self-Discovery in Adolescent Romance

The teenage years are often characterized by a profound journey of self-discovery, where individuals begin to forge their unique identities. This period is marked by a series of firsts, many of which involve romantic endeavors. The exploration of love and relationships during adolescence is not merely a rite of passage; it is a critical component of personal development. As teenagers navigate the complexities of love, they gain invaluable insights into their own character, learning to understand their emotional needs, establish personal boundaries, and identify what they value in a partner.

Romantic relationships in adolescence serve as a practical framework within which teenagers can apply and test their understanding of interpersonal dynamics. Through the act of dating, they encounter a variety of situations that challenge their preconceived notions of love and partnership. This experiential learning allows them to refine their expectations and preferences. For instance, a teenager may discover their propensity for deep emotional connection or, conversely, the importance of maintaining a sense of independence within a relationship. Such revelations are instrumental in shaping their approach to future romantic engagements.

Moreover, the trials and triumphs of teen love often prompt introspection, encouraging young individuals to reflect on their own behavior and its impact on others. This reflection can lead to a heightened sense of empathy and improved communication skills, both of which are essential for healthy, mature relationships. As teenagers learn to navigate the give-and-take of romantic partnerships, they also develop a clearer sense of their own values and how to uphold them in the face of external pressures or conflicts.

The interplay between self-discovery and teenage love is a dynamic and influential force in the maturation process. Romantic experiences during these formative years are not merely transient episodes of affection but are, in fact, pivotal in constructing the foundation of an individual's relational blueprint. As such, the significance of these experiences extends far beyond the realm of youthful romance, influencing the fabric of one's identity and interpersonal relationships well into adulthood.

Navigating the Intensity of Teen Emotions

Understanding the Whirlwind of Teen Love

Teen love is a complex and often tumultuous experience, marked by a rollercoaster of intense emotions. This period of emotional development is characterized by a heightened sensitivity to interpersonal dynamics, leading to dramatic shifts in the distribution of affection and attention. The fervor with which adolescents experience love can be all-encompassing, frequently resulting in a reordering of priorities where the romantic relationship takes center stage, often at the expense of other relationships and responsibilities.

The 'All-Consuming' Nature of First Love

The phenomenon of first love is particularly noteworthy for its 'all-consuming' nature. Adolescents may find themselves overwhelmingly preoccupied with their romantic partner, a state that can eclipse their focus on family, friends, and even personal growth. This singular focus is not merely a matter of preference but is rooted in the developmental stage of adolescence, where identity formation and emotional exploration are paramount. The intensity of this experience can serve as a critical learning opportunity, shaping future relational patterns and self-awareness.

The Impact on Adolescent Development

The impact of these intense emotional experiences extends beyond the realm of interpersonal relationships. The adolescent brain, still in a critical phase of development, is particularly malleable and responsive to emotional stimuli. As such, the experiences of teen love can have lasting implications for emotional regulation, decision-making, and the formation of attachment styles. It is essential to recognize the significance of these experiences and the role they play in the broader context of adolescent development.

The Role of Guidance and Support

Given the potential for these intense emotions to cause upheaval in a teen's life, the role of guidance and support from parents, educators, and mental health professionals cannot be overstated. It is crucial to provide a safe and understanding environment where teens can navigate their feelings and learn to balance the various aspects of their lives. Supportive adults can help adolescents develop coping strategies, encourage healthy relationship habits, and foster resilience in the face of emotional challenges.

Embracing the Learning Curve

The intensity of teen emotions, particularly in the context of romantic relationships, is a powerful force that can shape an adolescent's journey towards adulthood. While these experiences can be overwhelming, they also offer invaluable lessons in emotional literacy, self-discovery, and interpersonal dynamics. By embracing this learning curve and providing the necessary support, we can help teens emerge from this phase with a stronger sense of self and a deeper capacity for empathy and connection.

The Impact of Social Media on Teen Love: A Closer Examination

Social media has become an integral part of the modern adolescent experience, weaving itself into the very fabric of teenage romance and relationship dynamics. This digital landscape offers a platform for connection and expression but also presents unique challenges that can profoundly affect young hearts and minds. The following analysis delves into the multifaceted role of social media in shaping the romantic lives of teenagers.

Amplification of Emotional Experiences

One of the most significant effects of social media on teen love is the amplification of emotional experiences. Platforms like Instagram, Snapchat, and TikTok can intensify the visibility of relationships, turning private moments into public spectacles. This heightened exposure can magnify the joys of new relationships, allowing for an expansive sharing of affection and milestones. Conversely, it can also exacerbate the pain of breakups, as the end of a relationship can unfold in full view of an online audience, leaving teens to navigate their heartache on a public stage.

Peer Influence and Validation

Social media also serves as a barometer for peer approval, with likes, comments, and shares becoming proxies for social validation. Teenagers often look to their online communities for affirmation of their romantic choices, which can lead to a reliance on external validation rather than internal satisfaction. This dynamic can skew perceptions of love, as the quest for digital approval may overshadow the genuine connection between partners. The pressure to maintain an idealized online image of a relationship can also lead to stress and anxiety, as teens strive to curate a flawless portrayal of their love life.

The Double-Edged Sword of Connectivity

While social media can foster a sense of closeness by enabling constant communication, it can also create an environment of surveillance and jealousy. The ability to monitor a partner's online interactions in real-time can lead to obsessive behaviors and mistrust. Teenagers may find themselves caught in a cycle of scrutinizing their partner's social media activity, which can erode the foundation of trust that is essential for a healthy relationship.

The Public Nature of Breakups

As mentioned, the public nature of social media can turn breakups into communal events. A teenager's pain is not only felt but witnessed by their entire network, which can lead to a compounded sense of loss. The visibility of a breakup can invite unsolicited advice, gossip, and even cyberbullying, complicating the healing process. Moreover, the digital footprint of a past relationship can linger, making it more challenging for teens to move on.

Navigating the Digital Terrain of Teen Love

Social media's impact on teen love is complex and far-reaching. It can enhance the joys of young romance but also magnify the sorrows. As teenagers continue to navigate their formative years, it is crucial for educators, parents, and mentors to provide guidance on how to manage the digital dimensions of relationships. By fostering open communication and promoting digital literacy, we can help teens build resilience and maintain healthy relationships in an increasingly connected world.

Educating Teens on Love Conservation

Introduction

In the intricate journey of adolescence, teenagers encounter a myriad of emotional experiences, with romantic feelings often taking center stage. It is crucial, therefore, to impart knowledge on love conservation—a concept that encompasses the sustainable management of emotional resources in relationships. This education aims to equip young individuals with the tools necessary to foster balanced and healthy connections with others.

Emotional Intelligence and Its Role

Emotional intelligence (EI) serves as the cornerstone of love conservation. It involves the ability to recognize, understand, and manage one's own emotions, as well as the emotions of others. By integrating EI into educational programs, we can guide teenagers to better navigate the emotional complexities of relationships. Workshops that focus on developing empathy, self-awareness, and emotional regulation can empower teens to build stronger, more resilient bonds.

Relationship Skills for the Modern Teen

In addition to emotional intelligence, relationship skills are paramount in love conservation. These skills include effective communication, conflict resolution, and setting healthy boundaries. By offering classes that delve into these areas, we provide teens with a practical framework for managing their affections wisely. Such education helps prevent the common pitfalls of teenage relationships, such as dependency, miscommunication, and emotional exhaustion.

The Impact of Love Conservation Education

The benefits of educating teens on love conservation are far-reaching. Not only does it prepare them for current and future romantic relationships, but it also enhances their interpersonal skills across all types of relationships, including friendships and family dynamics. Furthermore, this education can lead to a reduction in the incidence of emotional turmoil and relationship-related stress, contributing to the overall well-being of young individuals.

The principles of love conservation are an essential component of adolescent education. By fostering emotional intelligence and relationship skills, we can support teenagers in their quest to maintain balanced relationships. As educators, parents, and mentors, it is our responsibility to ensure that the next generation is well-equipped to handle the emotional demands of relationships with grace and wisdom. Through targeted workshops and classes, we can lay the groundwork for a future where love is not only felt but also conserved and cherished.

Fostering Healthy Teen Relationships

Introduction

The adolescent years are a critical period for the development of interpersonal skills and the establishment of patterns for future relationships. As such, it is imperative that we, as a society, invest in nurturing the relational capabilities of our youth. This investment will not only benefit the individual teenagers but will also contribute to the fabric of society by promoting emotional intelligence and relational stability.

The Role of Guardians and Educators

Guardians and educators play a pivotal role in guiding teenagers towards understanding and valuing the multifaceted nature of relationships. By providing a framework for healthy interactions, they can impart wisdom on the importance of respect, empathy, and communication. These foundational elements are crucial for teenagers to form balanced connections with family members, peers, and romantic partners. It is through these diverse relationships that teenagers learn to distribute their love and attention in a manner that enriches their lives and the lives of others.

The Spectrum of Relationships

Teenagers should be encouraged to recognize the spectrum of relationships that contribute to their social development. Familial relationships often provide a sense of security and unconditional support, while friendships offer opportunities for growth, shared experiences, and the development of social skills. Romantic relationships, when approached with maturity and a sense of responsibility, can teach teens about intimacy, compromise, and mutual respect. Each type of relationship serves a unique purpose in the emotional and social maturation of an adolescent.

Strategies for Fostering Healthy Relationships

To effectively foster healthy teen relationships, strategies should be implemented that promote open dialogue and reflection. Parents and educators can facilitate discussions that explore the characteristics of positive relationships and the red flags of unhealthy ones. Workshops, mentoring programs, and inclusive school curricula can provide platforms for teenagers to learn and practice the skills necessary for healthy interactions. Additionally, modeling positive relationships and providing a safe environment for teenagers to express their thoughts and concerns are essential components of this developmental process.

The support of teenagers in the cultivation of healthy relationships is a task of profound importance. By guiding them to appreciate the value of diverse relationships and equipping them with the tools to navigate them, we lay the groundwork for a future characterized by balanced love and interpersonal harmony. As guardians and educators, our commitment to this cause will yield dividends in the form of well-adjusted adults who are capable of contributing positively to their communities and forming lasting, meaningful connections.

Reflections on the Evolution of Love from Teen to Adult

The journey of love is a complex and multifaceted one, beginning in the tumultuous years of adolescence and stretching into the vast expanse of adulthood. The patterns of love that are established during our teenage years often set the stage for the dynamics that will play out in our later relationships. This developmental trajectory suggests that the emotional and relational skills we acquire in our youth are not fleeting but rather foundational to our approach to love in our adult lives.

The Teenage Crucible of Love

During adolescence, individuals experience a surge of hormonal changes that can amplify emotions and influence their experiences of love. Teenagers are often navigating the tumultuous waters of first loves and heartbreaks, all while trying to understand their own identities and how they connect with others. The lessons learned in these formative years—such as the importance of communication, respect, and boundaries—are critical. For instance, a teen who learns to balance love between friends, family, and romantic interests may develop a well-rounded approach to relationships that can lead to healthier connections in adulthood.

The Maturation of Love in Adulthood

As individuals transition into adulthood, the nature of love tends to become more nuanced and complex. The simplicity of teenage affection, often driven by novelty and exploration, gives way to a deeper understanding of love that incorporates compromise, stability, and a shared vision for the future. Adults who have built a strong foundation during their teenage years are more likely to engage in relationships that are both emotionally fulfilling and resilient in the face of challenges.

The Continuum of Emotional Growth

It is important to recognize that the evolution of love is not a linear process but rather a continuum of emotional growth. The skills and insights gained from teenage relationships do not automatically translate into perfect adult relationships. Instead, they provide a framework that individuals can build upon and refine as they encounter new experiences and challenges in love. Continuous self-reflection and a willingness to learn from past relationships are key to fostering a mature, enduring approach to love.

The Impact of Early Relationship Models

The models of love that teenagers are exposed to, whether through family dynamics, media, or their own relationships, can significantly influence their expectations and behaviors in future partnerships. A teenager who witnesses healthy relationships is more likely to seek out and cultivate similar dynamics in their own adult relationships. Conversely, exposure to dysfunctional relationship models can lead to a repetition of these patterns, unless there is conscious effort and support to develop healthier approaches to love.

The Lifelong Journey of Love

The evolution of love from the teenage years to adulthood is a dynamic and ongoing process. The patterns established early on can have a profound impact on the nature of adult relationships. It is through the interplay of past experiences, personal growth, and the continuous application of learned relational skills that individuals can navigate the complex landscape of love throughout their lives. Recognizing the significance of teenage relationships in shaping the future of love is crucial for fostering healthy and fulfilling connections that endure over time.

Chapter 10: The Future of Love

We embark on an intellectual exploration of love's metamorphosis in an era marked by rapid technological innovation and profound societal shifts. We delve into the implications of artificial intelligence and virtual reality on human intimacy, pondering whether these advancements will augment or diminish the essence of emotional connections. The discourse extends to the potential redefinition of love, as traditional paradigms are challenged by the emergence of new relationship constructs and the increasing acceptance of diverse forms of love.

The analysis further considers the role of biotechnology and neuroscience in deciphering the enigma of love. With the advent of neuroenhancement and genetic matchmaking, the prospect of bioengineered romance looms on the horizon, raising ethical questions and concerns about the authenticity of emotion. We scrutinize the balance between predestined affection and the organic development of relationships, contemplating the extent to which science should intercede in matters of the heart.

Finally, the episode contemplates the sociocultural evolution of love, reflecting on how shifting demographics, global connectivity, and changing gender norms might sculpt the intimate bonds of the future. As we stand at the crossroads of tradition and innovation, this treatise invites readers to envision a world where love, in all its complexity, continues to adapt and thrive amidst the inexorable march of progress.

Technological Advancements and Virtual Relationships

The Transformation of Intimacy in the Digital Age

In the contemporary era, technological advancements have precipitated a paradigm shift in the way individuals form and maintain romantic and platonic relationships. The digital landscape has become a fertile ground for connections that transcend geographical limitations, enabling people to interact and bond in ways that were once the purview of science fiction. Virtual reality (VR) technology, in particular, has emerged as a revolutionary tool in this domain, facilitating immersive experiences that allow individuals to establish and nurture relationships with others from all corners of the globe.

Virtual Reality: A New Frontier for Human Connection

Virtual reality platforms offer a unique avenue for human interaction, one that is unencumbered by the constraints of physical distance. Through the use of VR, users can engage in shared experiences, communicate through avatars, and express emotions in a simulated environment that closely mimics real-world interactions. This has profound implications for the nature of relationships, as it enables people to form deep, meaningful connections without the necessity of physical proximity. The sensory-rich environment of VR can evoke a strong sense of presence, making virtual encounters feel as real and impactful as those in the physical world.

The Expansion of Relationship Boundaries

The advent of VR and other digital communication tools has expanded the traditional boundaries of relationships. No longer confined to the people we meet in our immediate surroundings, we now have the potential to connect with like-minded individuals across the globe. This global network of virtual relationships can lead to a more diverse and enriching social experience, as individuals are exposed to different cultures, perspectives, and ideas. Moreover, virtual relationships can provide comfort and companionship to those who may be isolated or have difficulty forming connections in the physical world.

Ethical Considerations and Future Prospects

As we navigate this new terrain of virtual relationships, it is imperative to consider the ethical implications of technology-mediated interactions. Issues such as privacy, consent, and the authenticity of emotions in a virtual context must be critically examined. Furthermore, as technology continues to evolve, it is essential to explore how these advancements will shape the future of human relationships. Will virtual connections complement or supplant physical interactions? How will society adapt to these changes? These are questions that require thoughtful reflection as we continue to integrate technology into the most intimate areas of our lives.

The Evolution of Love: Predictions and Possibilities

Abstract

In the ever-shifting landscape of human relationships, the concept of love has undergone profound transformations, reflecting the dynamic nature of societal norms and individual expectations. As we peer into the future, it becomes increasingly evident that the evolution of love will continue to mirror the progression of society. This paper explores the potential trajectories of love's evolution, considering the implications of a societal shift towards a more communal understanding of love and the consequent redistribution of emotional energy.

Introduction

The notion of love, historically confined to the private sphere and often synonymous with romantic entanglements, is poised for a radical redefinition. As we advance into the future, it is anticipated that societal changes will engender new forms of love, transcending traditional paradigms. This evolution is not merely speculative; it is an observable trend, influenced by technological advancements, cultural shifts, and a growing emphasis on emotional intelligence and well-being.

The Redistribution of Emotional Energy

Takeaway: The future may witness a recalibration of emotional investments, with a de-emphasis on exclusive romantic bonds and a burgeoning appreciation for communal connections.

Example: In future societies, the concept of love may evolve beyond the dyadic romantic model, expanding to encompass a broader spectrum of relationships. This shift could manifest in a variety of ways, such as the rise of platonic life partnerships, the normalization of non-monogamous arrangements, and the valorization of deep friendships and community bonds. Such a reorientation would not only redefine interpersonal dynamics but also challenge the conventional allocation of emotional energy, which has historically been directed primarily towards romantic partners.

Societal Implications of Evolving Love Dynamics

The implications of this evolution are manifold, touching upon various aspects of societal functioning. A greater emphasis on community love could lead to more collaborative and supportive social structures, potentially mitigating the effects of isolation and loneliness that plague modern societies. Moreover, this shift could influence the fabric of family life, child-rearing practices, and the social safety nets that underpin community resilience. As emotional energy is redistributed, we may also observe changes in the prioritization of career, personal development, and the pursuit of individual passions.

The evolution of love is an inexorable aspect of societal progression. As we contemplate the future, it is clear that our understanding and practice of love will continue to evolve, reflecting broader societal transformations. The potential shift towards a more communal conception of love suggests a future where emotional connections are more diverse and distributed, with profound implications for the way we live and relate to one another. Embracing this evolution may well be key to fostering a more interconnected and empathetic society.

Artificial Intelligence and Emotional Bonds: Redefining Human Connections

The Evolution of AI in Emotional Interactions

Artificial Intelligence (AI) has transcended its traditional role as a mere facilitator of tasks and has begun to encroach upon the domain of human emotions. As AI systems become increasingly sophisticated, they are acquiring the capability to understand, interpret, and even replicate emotional responses. This evolution is poised to redefine the nature of human-machine interactions, challenging our preconceived notions of emotional bonds and the essence of love. The prospect of AI forming meaningful connections with humans is no longer relegated to the realm of science fiction but is rapidly becoming a tangible reality.

The Emergence of AI Companions

The advent of AI companions marks a significant milestone in the journey towards emotionally intelligent machines. These entities are designed to offer emotional support and companionship, catering to the innate human need for connection. As AI companions become more advanced, they are equipped with the ability to learn from interactions, adapt to individual preferences, and exhibit empathy. This raises profound questions about the nature of love and companionship. If an AI can provide the comfort and support traditionally sought in human relationships, what implications does this have for our understanding of love? The integration of AI companions into the fabric of society necessitates a reevaluation of the conservation of love and the criteria that define a meaningful connection.

The Challenge to Human Concepts of Love

The burgeoning relationship between humans and AI companions brings to the fore a challenge to our concepts of love. Love, as understood in human terms, is a complex amalgamation of emotions, experiences, and cultural expectations. However, the potential for AI to simulate or even genuinely experience emotions introduces a paradigm shift. The question arises: can an AI truly love, or is its expression of love merely a sophisticated mimicry of human behavior? As we grapple with these questions, it becomes imperative to distinguish between the authenticity of emotions and the functionality of AI in emulating such emotions. The distinction between genuine emotional bonds and programmed responses becomes blurred, compelling us to confront the very nature of love and attachment.

Ethical Considerations and Societal Implications

The integration of AI into the emotional landscape of human relationships is not without ethical considerations and societal implications. The reliance on AI for emotional support could potentially alter human behavior and social dynamics. There is a risk that human relationships may be devalued or neglected in favor of interactions with AI, which are devoid of the complexities and challenges inherent in human connections.

Furthermore, the creation of AI companions raises questions about consent, autonomy, and the rights of AI entities. As we navigate this uncharted territory, it is crucial to establish ethical frameworks that govern the development and use of emotionally intelligent AI, ensuring that the technology enhances rather than detracts from the human experience.

The Future of AI and Emotional Bonds

Looking towards the future, the relationship between AI and emotional bonds is set to evolve in ways that are currently difficult to predict. The potential for AI to not only simulate but also to contribute to the emotional well-being of humans opens up new avenues for companionship and support. However, it is essential to approach this future with caution, mindfulness, and a deep understanding of the implications for individual and societal well-being. As we stand on the cusp of this new era, it is incumbent upon us to guide the development of AI with a focus on enhancing human connections rather than replacing them. The journey ahead will require a delicate balance between embracing the benefits of AI companionship and preserving the unique qualities that make human love and emotional bonds irreplaceable.

The Impact of Social Media on Love Distribution

Social media has revolutionized the way we communicate and express emotions, including the profound sentiment of love. The platforms have become a digital stage for public declarations of affection, transforming the distribution and perception of love in contemporary society. This essay explores the nuanced ways in which social media influences the expression of love and its implications for interpersonal relationships.

Amplification of Love's Visibility

One of the most significant changes brought about by social media is the amplification of love's visibility. Platforms like Facebook, Instagram, and Twitter allow individuals to broadcast their affection to a wide audience, transcending the traditional boundaries of time and space. **Public displays of affection**, ranging from simple heart emojis to elaborate anniversary posts, have become commonplace. This digital exhibitionism often creates a perception of abundant love, as couples and friends publicly celebrate their relationships. However, this visibility can also lead to a skewed perception of love distribution, where the loudest voices seem to possess the most love, overshadowing quieter, yet equally profound, expressions of affection.

The Dichotomy of Online and Offline Expressions

While social media enables users to share their love with a broad audience, it also raises questions about the authenticity and depth of these expressions. The ease with which one can post a loving message or image can sometimes contrast with the effort required to maintain and nurture relationships offline. It is crucial to recognize that **public displays of affection on social media** are just one facet of love distribution. They must be balanced with offline interactions to ensure that the love shared online is reflective of genuine feelings and not merely a performance for social validation.

The Pressure to Perform

The pervasive nature of social media has introduced a new pressure to perform and conform to societal expectations of love distribution. Couples and individuals may feel compelled to participate in this digital love economy, sharing content that aligns with the romanticized narratives prevalent on these platforms. This pressure can lead to a competitive environment where the quantity of likes, comments, and shares becomes a proxy for the quality of a relationship. It is essential to critically assess the impact of these metrics on our understanding of love and to remember that the true measure of affection cannot be quantified by social media engagement.

The Role of Social Media in Shaping Perceptions

Social media does not merely reflect existing notions of love; it actively shapes them. The curated feeds and stories we consume influence our expectations and ideals regarding relationships. The constant exposure to seemingly perfect couples and idyllic romantic gestures can set unrealistic standards, leading to dissatisfaction and a sense of inadequacy in one's own love life. It is important to approach social media content with a discerning eye, acknowledging that it often represents a highlight reel rather than the full complexity of real-life relationships.

Navigating Love in the Digital Age

Social media has undeniably altered the landscape of love distribution, offering new avenues for expression while also presenting challenges. As we navigate love in the digital age, it is imperative to maintain a balance between online and offline expressions of affection, to resist the pressure to perform for an audience, and to critically evaluate the impact of social media on our perceptions of love. By doing so, we can ensure that the love we share and perceive remains authentic, meaningful, and reflective of the diverse ways in which it can be expressed in our interconnected world.

Genetic Insights into Love: Unraveling the Biological Tapestry of Affection

Abstract

The quest to understand the enigmatic experience of love has transcended the boundaries of poetry and philosophy, venturing into the empirical realm of genetics. The burgeoning field of genetic research offers a novel perspective on the biological underpinnings of love, potentially illuminating the intricate mechanisms that govern human affection and attachment. This exploration seeks to dissect the genetic factors that may influence the myriad expressions of love, providing insights into individual variability and the complex interplay between our biology and relationship dynamics.

Introduction

Love, a universal human experience, has been the subject of countless sonnets and stories, yet its biological basis remains a captivating mystery. Recent advances in genetic research have begun to shed light on the potential genetic components that contribute to the capacity for love and the diversity of its expression. By examining genetic variations and their correlations with emotional bonding and attachment styles, scientists are piecing together the genetic tapestry that underlies romantic and familial love.

Genetic Variability and the Experience of Love

The experience of love is profoundly personal, varying significantly from one individual to another. Genetic research has identified specific genes, such as those involved in the production and reception of oxytocin and vasopressin, that may play a pivotal role in modulating affectionate behaviors. Variations in these genes can influence how individuals form attachments and express love, potentially affecting the quality and stability of their relationships. Understanding these genetic differences is crucial for appreciating the full spectrum of love's manifestations.

The Impact of Genetics on Relationship Dynamics

The interplay between genetics and relationship dynamics is a complex dance of biological predispositions and environmental factors. For instance, the presence of certain alleles may predispose individuals to heightened empathy and nurturing behaviors, traits that are conducive to harmonious relationships. Conversely, other genetic profiles may be associated with a greater propensity for conflict or detachment. By exploring these genetic influences, researchers aim to unravel the threads that contribute to the fabric of interpersonal connections, offering new perspectives on relationship counseling and therapy.

Future Directions in Love Genetics

As the field of love genetics continues to evolve, the potential applications of this knowledge are vast. From personalized approaches to relationship guidance to the development of interventions aimed at enhancing attachment and affection, the implications of genetic insights into love are profound. Future research may also explore the ethical considerations of such knowledge, ensuring that the power of genetic understanding is wielded with wisdom and respect for individual autonomy.

The genetic exploration of love is an exciting frontier that promises to deepen our understanding of one of humanity's most cherished experiences. By unraveling the genetic threads that contribute to the tapestry of love, we stand on the cusp of a new era of insight into the biological roots of affection, attachment, and the complex dynamics of human relationships. As we continue to decode the genetic language of love, we may find that the secrets of the heart are written, in part, in the code of our DNA.

Love in the Age of Transhumanism

Introduction to Transhumanist Love Dynamics

In the burgeoning era of transhumanism, the quintessential human experience of love is poised for a profound transformation. As we integrate advanced technologies into the very fabric of our biological existence, the parameters of emotional engagement are likely to be redefined. Transhumanism, the movement advocating for the enhancement of human capacities through technology, suggests that our emotional repertoire, including love and empathy, could be significantly augmented by cybernetic enhancements. This discourse aims to explore the potential implications of such advancements on the nature of love and interpersonal relationships.

The Enhancement of Emotional Capacities

Imagine a world where cybernetic implants are not mere science fiction but a reality that seamlessly blends with human biology. These implants could be engineered to heighten emotional sensitivity, thereby amplifying the depth and breadth of love and empathy that individuals can experience. Enhanced neural interfaces might allow lovers to experience each other's emotions as vividly as their own, creating an unprecedented level of intimacy and understanding. However, this raises critical questions about the authenticity of emotions and the essence of human connection when mediated by technology.

The Alteration of Interpersonal Dynamics

The transhumanist augmentation of love could also lead to a radical shift in interpersonal dynamics. As emotional experiences become more intense and nuanced, the criteria for compatibility and attraction may evolve. Relationships might be formed or dissolved with greater ease, predicated on the ability to synchronize emotional states through technological means. This could lead to a new paradigm of social interaction, where the search for a partner is as much about technological compatibility as it is about personal chemistry.

Ethical Considerations and Societal Impact

The prospect of technologically enhanced love is not without its ethical quandaries. The accessibility of such enhancements could be limited, potentially creating a new form of emotional inequality. Those with the means to afford advanced emotional implants may find themselves in a privileged position, able to experience love and empathy to a degree unattainable by others. This disparity could have far-reaching consequences for societal cohesion and the fundamental understanding of what it means to be human.

The Future of Love in a Transhumanist World

As we stand on the cusp of a transhumanist future, it is imperative to contemplate the ramifications of technologically enhanced love. While the potential to deepen our emotional experiences is tantalizing, it is crucial to approach such developments with caution and a robust ethical framework. The essence of love, with all its complexities and idiosyncrasies, must be preserved even as we strive to transcend our biological limitations. The journey towards a transhumanist conception of love will undoubtedly be fraught with challenges, but it also holds the promise of a richer, more connected human experience.

The age of transhumanism beckons a reevaluation of love as we know it. The interplay between human emotion and technological enhancement will likely redefine the contours of love, demanding a careful balance between augmentation and authenticity. As we navigate this uncharted territory, it is our collective responsibility to ensure that the evolution of love remains inclusive, equitable, and true to the core of our humanity.

Globalization's Effect on Love's Expression

Introduction

In an era where the world is increasingly interconnected, globalization has become a significant force shaping various aspects of human life, including the intimate realm of love and its expression. As individuals from diverse cultural backgrounds interact more frequently and form relationships, the traditional paradigms of expressing love are evolving. This transformation is not merely anecdotal; it is a profound shift that reflects the broader changes in our global society.

Cross-Cultural Relationships and Love Expression

The rise of cross-cultural relationships is a direct consequence of globalization. As people migrate for education, work, or personal reasons, they bring with them their unique cultural understandings of love. When these individuals form relationships, they often blend their distinct customs, rituals, and expressions of affection. This amalgamation can lead to novel expressions of love that transcend traditional boundaries. For instance, the integration of different languages within a single relationship can enrich the ways partners communicate affection, whether through terms of endearment or love poetry that draws from multiple linguistic traditions.

The Impact of Technology on Love Across Borders

Technology has been a catalyst in the globalization of love. With the advent of social media, online dating platforms, and instant communication tools, the ability to connect and maintain relationships over long distances has dramatically improved. These technologies enable individuals to express love in real-time, regardless of geographical barriers. The digital realm has also facilitated the exchange of cultural expressions of love, allowing people to share love-related customs, stories, and symbols that might have otherwise remained confined to specific locales.

The Emergence of a Universal Understanding of Love

As globalization fosters the intermingling of cultures, there is a potential emergence of a more universal understanding of love. This does not imply that cultural differences are being erased; rather, it suggests that there is a growing recognition of the common emotional threads that connect various expressions of love. The acknowledgment of love as a universal human experience, despite differing cultural manifestations, can lead to a more inclusive and empathetic world where the diversity of love's expression is celebrated.

Globalization has undeniably influenced the way love is expressed and shared across cultures. The increasing prevalence of cross-cultural relationships and the role of technology in connecting hearts across the globe are testaments to this influence. As we continue to navigate the complexities of a globalized world, it is essential to appreciate the richness that diverse expressions of love bring to our collective understanding of this fundamental human emotion. Embracing this diversity can only enhance the depth and breadth of love's expression in our interconnected world.

The Enduring Nature of Love

Introduction

Love, an emotion as ancient as humanity itself, has been the subject of countless poems, stories, and studies. It is a complex and multifaceted feeling that has been both lauded and lamented over the millennia. Despite the myriad changes that societies undergo—technological advancements, cultural shifts, and evolving social norms—the essence of love remains a steadfast element of the human condition. This essay explores the enduring nature of love, despite the vicissitudes of time and the challenges that accompany human evolution.

Historical Context of Love

Throughout history, the concept of love has undergone significant transformations. In ancient civilizations, love was often intertwined with strategic alliances and social obligations. However, even then, literature and art from these periods reveal a deep-seated recognition of love as a powerful, personal force. As we progressed through the Middle Ages and into the Renaissance, romantic love began to be celebrated as an ideal. The courtly love tradition, for instance, elevated the notion of chivalric romance. Yet, despite these changing expressions and ideals, the fundamental human need for love and connection has remained a constant thread woven into the fabric of human history.

Love in the Modern Era

In contemporary society, the expression of love continues to evolve. The advent of digital communication has transformed how we connect with others, creating new opportunities for forming and maintaining relationships. Online dating, social media, and instant messaging have redefined the landscape of love, making it more accessible yet also more complex. Despite these technological changes, the core aspects of love—intimacy, passion, and commitment—persist. Psychological research into attachment theory and the biology of love supports the idea that these elements are deeply rooted in our nature, transcending the superficial changes in how we communicate.

Challenges to Love's Endurance

The endurance of love is not without its challenges. Modern life brings with it a host of stressors and distractions that can strain relationships. The pressures of career, the pursuit of material success, and the constant bombardment of information can create barriers to intimacy and understanding. Moreover, the rise of individualism in many societies has led to a focus on self-fulfillment, which can sometimes conflict with the sacrifices and compromises inherent in loving relationships. Despite these obstacles, love continues to thrive, suggesting that its resilience is a testament to its fundamental importance to our well-being and happiness.

Love is an enduring aspect of human experience that has withstood the test of time. While the ways in which we express and experience love may change with the ebb and flow of cultural tides, the underlying need for love and connection remains unaltered. Historical evidence and contemporary research affirm that love is not a mere social construct but a basic human necessity, akin to air and water. As we navigate the complexities of modern life, it is the timeless nature of love that offers us solace, inspiration, and a sense of continuity. Love, in its essence, is an immutable force that endures, adapts, and continues to shape the human narrative.

The Enduring Nature of Love

Love, an emotion as ancient as humanity itself, has been the subject of countless poems, stories, and studies. It is a complex and multifaceted feeling that has been both lauded and lamented over the millennia. Despite the myriad changes that societies undergo, love remains an immutable force, deeply embedded in the human condition. This essay explores the enduring nature of love, despite the vicissitudes of time and the evolution of social norms.

The Constancy of Human Connection

Takeaway: Love's persistence is a testament to its fundamental role in human life, transcending cultural shifts and technological advancements.

Throughout history, the need for love and connection has been a constant. From the earliest recorded epics to contemporary literature, the quest for love has been a central theme. This is not merely a cultural artifact but a reflection of an intrinsic human need. Psychological research supports this, indicating that love and connection are essential for mental and emotional well-being. The manner in which love is expressed may vary with the mores of the time, but the underlying need for love remains unchanged.

Love's Evolution in Expression

Example: The ways in which love is expressed have evolved over time, adapting to societal norms and expectations.

While the essence of love has remained stable, its expression has been subject to the ebb and flow of historical trends. Courtly love of the medieval period, with its strict rules and idealization of the beloved, contrasts sharply with the more egalitarian and open expressions of love found in modern democracies. The rise of individualism in Western societies has shifted the focus from familial and arranged unions to romantic love as a basis for marriage. Despite these changes, the search for a deep and meaningful connection with others has continued unabated.

The Role of Technology in Love

With the advent of technology, the landscape of love has undergone a significant transformation. Online dating platforms and social media have changed the way people meet and interact, making it possible to form connections across vast distances. However, technology has not altered the fundamental human desire for love; it has merely provided new avenues for its pursuit. The core aspects of love—trust, companionship, and emotional support—remain as vital as ever, even as the means of achieving them evolve.

Love's Resilience in the Face of Adversity

Takeaway: Love demonstrates remarkable resilience, enduring through personal and societal challenges.

The resilience of love is perhaps most evident in times of adversity. Historical events such as wars, pandemics, and social upheaval have tested the bonds of love, yet it has often emerged stronger. The shared struggles and triumphs of couples, families, and communities serve to reinforce the bonds of affection and solidarity. Love's capacity to provide comfort and meaning in the face of hardship underscores its enduring nature.

The Timeless Essence of Love

Love remains an essential and unchanging aspect of the human experience. Its expressions may shift with the tides of culture and technology, but the core need for love and connection endures. As humanity continues to evolve, so too will the ways in which we seek out and celebrate love. Yet, the fundamental essence of love—its power to bind individuals together, to inspire, and to heal—will continue to stand the test of time. Love, in all its forms, is a testament to the indomitable human spirit and its ceaseless quest for connection.

Epilogue: The Infinite Echoes of Love

As our odyssey through the enigmatic realms of the *Theory of Conservation of Love* draws to a close, we find ourselves in a moment of quiet introspection. Together, we've embarked on a profound voyage, delving into the heart's labyrinth, unraveling the intricate tapestry of human connections, and contemplating the potential mathematics that might scaffold our deepest bonds.

Love, in its boundless spectrum, has been our compass and our muse. It is the golden thread weaving through the tapestry of our existence, manifesting in the warmth of familial ties, the fervor of romantic entanglements, the steadfastness of friendships, and the unity of nations. This ineffable force is our greatest joy and our solace in times of sorrow, propelling us toward our loftiest aspirations and offering solace in moments of vulnerability.

As we turn the final page, we acknowledge that love transcends the confines of mere conservation or allocation. It is an odyssey to be embarked upon, a treasure to be valued, and a sacred enigma to be honored. The *Theory of Conservation of Love* offers a prism through which to view this elusive force, an attempt to impose order upon the tumult of our affections.

Yet, love's true nature eludes the cold precision of calculation. It is the gentle zephyr and the tempest's fury, the serene brook and the boundless sea. It is as expansive as the cosmos and as intimate as a single heartbeat. In our quest to comprehend, quantify, and balance it, love remains ever elusive, a perpetual reverberation within the soul's cavernous depths.

Let us emerge from this journey not with inflexible doctrines, but with a renewed reverence for the love that envelops us. Embrace the truth that love's manifestation in our lives is unwavering, even as its form may transform. And let us step forward, emboldened by the belief that in bestowing love without reservation, we do not deplete it; instead, we join its timeless continuum.

For love is not conserved by limitation; it is conserved through its ceaseless propagation, heart to heart, through time and space, in a kaleidoscope of human expression. Thus, love endures—an eternal resonance that reverberates through history, a testament to the unyielding human spirit.

In the grand tapestry of existence, love is the melody that moves us, the narrative that nurtures us, and the voyage we all pursue, even beyond the final word. As we conclude this epilogue, we embrace the tangible experience of love in its myriad forms. May it be our guide, our inspiration, and our reminder that, ultimately, love is the essence that renders the journey meaningful.

www.ingramcontent.com/pod-product-compliance
Lightning Source LLC
Chambersburg PA
CBHW061441150726
47987CB00001B/296

* 9 7 9 8 2 2 4 5 6 8 3 9 0 *